Am I Fat?
The Obesity Issue for Teens

ISSUES IN FOCUS TODAY

Kathlyn Gay

Enslow Publishers, Inc.

40 Industrial Road	PO Box 38
Box 398	Aldershot
Berkeley Heights, NJ 07922	Hants GU12 6BP
USA	UK

http://www.enslow.com

Library of Congress Cataloging-in-Publication Data

Gay, Kathlyn.
    Am I fat? : the obesity issue for teens / Kathlyn Gay.
       p. cm. — (Issues in focus today)
    Includes bibliographical references and index.
    ISBN-10: 0-7660-2527-6
    1. Obesity in adolescence—Juvenile literature. 2. Eating disorders in adolescence—
Juvenile literature. 3. Teenagers—Health and hygiene—Juvenile literature. I. Title.
II. Series.
    RJ399.C6G39 2006
    618.92'398—dc22

                                                       2005013412
ISBN-13: 978-0-7660-2527-1

Printed in the United States of America

10 9 8 7 6 5 4 3

To Our Readers:
We have done our best to make sure that all Internet Addresses in this book were active and
appropriate when we went to press. However, the author and publisher have no control over
and assume no liability for the material available on those Internet sites or on other Web sites
they may link to. Any comments or suggestions can be sent by e-mail to comments@enslow.com
or to the address on the back cover.

C o n t e n t s

Acknowledgments

*Thanks to those who assisted with research:
Nissa Beth Gay, Gina Fontana, Shyam Dahiya, M.D.,
Amelia Barcenas, and Veronica Salotto.
I'm indebted also to those who shared
their experiences and views about obesity
in media stories and medical journals.*

What Is Obesity?

When Christianne was thirteen years old, she weighed 180 pounds and faced daily taunts and jeers from classmates. "Kids at school called me stupid things like 'tub of lard' or 'fatty.' Some kids would yell 'Moo,'" she told a *Choices* reporter, adding, "It really hurt."[1]

Teenager Kendall Brasch, who weighed 265 pounds, said she had tried numerous diets to reduce her weight, but nothing worked, according to a report in the *Seattle Times*. In her words, "I was so depressed I didn't care about anything. I would go to school wearing pajamas, wouldn't talk to anyone and come home and sit in front of the TV."[2]

Like adolescent girls, boys also suffer when they are

overweight and say it is clear to them that being fat is not acceptable to their classmates. They describe incidents of harassment, such as being called "fatty-fatty-two-by-four," "army tank," or "gunboat." One young man told of being picked on at lunchtime, when others at his table threw food at him, calling him a pig and demanding that he eat the scraps or suffer a beating after school.

Whether male or female, some young people who are extremely overweight drop out of school and will not leave the house unless it is absolutely necessary. They may also be teased at home when brothers, sisters, or other relatives label them with humiliating terms: "fat chick," "orca," "big chops," and on and on. Early in their lives, they learn that those who are overweight are likely to be rejected. They become loners and have low self-esteem; they feel guilty because they cannot lose weight. Some say they reach a point where they hate to look at themselves in the mirror and dread buying clothes. Many teens tell about constant dieting or developing eating disorders in their efforts to control their weight.

On any given week, you can easily find a magazine or newspaper article, Internet posting, or television news report that tells about the pain experienced by children, teenagers, and adults who have been ridiculed, harassed, bullied, and sometimes physically assaulted because of weighing more, often much more, than their peers. In recent years, print and electronic media have also called attention to the health risks and economic costs of being fat—or in today's terminology, being overweight or obese.

Obesity

Although the terms *fat, overweight,* and *obese* are bandied about by the media, the words are not synonymous. In medical terminology, fat refers to the billions of fat cells in the body (40 billion in an average adult); these cells affect basic body functions. According to the U.S. National Institutes of Health (NIH):

Overweight refers to an excess of body weight compared to set standards. The excess weight may come from muscle, bone, fat, and/or body water. Obesity refers specifically to having an abnormally high proportion of body fat. A person can be overweight without being obese, as in the example of a bodybuilder or other athlete who has a lot of muscle. However, many people who are overweight are also obese.[3]

A medical encyclopedia simplifies the definition, stating that obesity means weighing 20 percent or more than is considered desirable for a person's height, age, gender, and bone structure.[4]

Such was the case for sixteen-year-old Amanda of suburban Pittsburgh, Pennsylvania, who was the subject of an ABC News report about obesity. Amanda, who weighed almost three hundred pounds at the time of the report, has struggled most of her life with her weight. As she explains, "There was a time I gained 20 pounds in one month, and I was 10 years old, and my doctor was like, 'Amanda, you can't do this.'" Amanda's father tried to help her by recommending diets and various programs advertised on TV. By the time she was twelve years old, Amanda had been on numerous diets and had attended sessions of Weight Watchers, a popular program for losing weight. But nothing worked. As she puts it, "I was always hungry."[5]

While the news report pointed out Amanda's and the doctors' concerns, it did not indicate how she might eventually lose weight—or if she can. There is little doubt, however, that unless she can shed pounds, she is at risk for life-threatening health problems such as heart disease and stroke. She already suffers from diabetes and liver disease. Obesity specialist Dr. Philip Schauer of Pittsburgh noted that "Teenagers who have a [weight] problem now—that continue to increase or stay the same in terms of their weight—will likely have a much higher risk of premature death."[6]

Steady Weight Gains

Since the 1960s, Americans and people in other industrialized countries generally have been gaining weight, data show. In fact,

Americans are the most overweight people in the world. The trend has steadily increased over the years among both genders, all ages, all racial/ethnic groups, and all educational levels. From 1960 to 2000, those considered overweight increased from 31.5 to 33.6 percent among U.S. adults aged twenty to seventy-four. During this same period, the percentage of obese adults more than doubled, from 13.3 to 30.9 percent, according to the most recent data from the NIH. The institute also reports that about 15.3 percent of children (ages six through eleven) and 15.5 percent of adolescents (ages twelve through nineteen) were overweight in 2000. An additional 15 percent of children and 14.9 percent of teenagers were at risk of becoming overweight. That is, they weighed more than other children and teens of the same gender and age as shown on growth charts from the U.S. Centers for Disease Control and Prevention (CDC).[7]

Similar increases have been recorded in Canada. A health survey released in 2004 showed that 13.6 percent of eighteen- and nineteen-year-olds there were overweight and 5.5 percent were obese. The proportions who were overweight increased with age: Among those aged twenty through twenty-four, 21.8 percent were overweight and 8.6 obese, and among older adults, including baby boomers, 37.9 percent were overweight and 18.5 percent were obese.[8]

These extra pounds are leading to chronic diseases and literally killing people. Indeed, the U.S. CDC declared in a 2004 study that obesity-related diseases would contribute to about four hundred thousand deaths annually, almost as many as those caused by smoking. Officials predicted that obesity would surpass the 435,000 deaths due to smoking and would soon be the leading cause of preventable death.

The *Journal of the American Medical Association* (*JAMA*) published the CDC study in its March 10, 2004 issue, but skeptics soon denounced the study as flawed. In late November 2004, the CDC acknowledged that the agency had made an error in its computer computations and that deaths due to obesity had been overestimated by tens of thousands. CDC officials said corrections would be published in the *JAMA* and apologized for the "unintentional error and any confusion it may have caused." In spite of the faulty numbers, CDC's chief of science pointed out that "we stand by the bottom-line message: Tobacco and obesity are the two major risk factors for preventable death in the United States."[9]

Body Mass Index

When health experts determine whether people are underweight, normal weight, overweight, or obese, they may use one of several methods. One is based on tables used for many years by insurance companies showing the desirable weight for one's height.

Another is based on measurements of skin-fold thickness, using calipers, a device that pinches the skin in various body locations, such as the upper arm, waist, and thigh. Calipers measure the thickness of a skin fold and its underlying fat, shown on a dial or digital readout. These measurements provide an estimate of the total amount of fat on a person's body. However, the accuracy of this method for measuring body fat depends on the skill of the person using the calipers.

Since the 1960s, Americans and people in other industrialized countries generally have been gaining weight, data show. The trend has steadily increased over the years among both genders, all ages, all racial/ethnic groups, and all educational levels.

The standard most commonly used today to learn whether a person's weight points to a health risk is the body mass index (BMI). Someone with a BMI of 18.5 to less than 25 is at a normal weight and at less risk for an illness than those who have a BMI of 25 to 29.9 (indicating overweight) or those who have a BMI of 30 or more (indicating obesity). Generally, adults can figure their BMI by using a chart or a general formula.

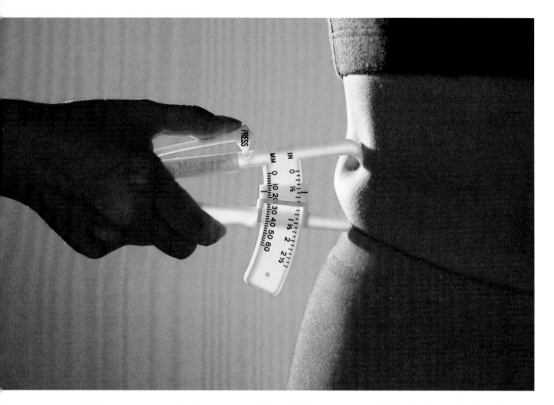

Calipers are used to measure the thickness of a fold of skin and the fat underneath it.

The BMI has limits, however. Muscular people such as athletes may fall into the "overweight" category but not have health risks because they are actually fit. People who have lost muscle mass, such as the elderly, may be in the "healthy weight" category—according to their BMI—when in fact they may be at risk for various ailments.

When measuring normal weight for children and teenagers, the BMI standards are different from those used for adults. As children grow, the fat stored in fat cells and organs of the body change. For example, a child might have a high proportion of fat weight at age eleven but have a lower proportion by age thirteen as he or she grows taller. Also, girls and boys differ in their body fat as they mature. So when determining BMI for children and

Body Mass Index

This table is for adults and is only an example of how BMI is determined. To use the table, find the appropriate height in the left-hand column labeled Height. Then move across to a given weight (in pounds). The number at the top of the column is the BMI at that height and weight. Pounds have been rounded off.

BMI	19	20	21	22	23	24	25	26	27	28	29	30	31	32	33	34	35
Height (inches)	Body weight (pounds)																
58	91	96	100	105	110	115	119	124	129	134	138	143	148	153	158	162	167
59	94	99	104	109	114	119	124	128	133	138	143	148	153	158	163	168	173
60	97	102	107	112	118	123	128	133	138	143	148	153	158	163	168	174	179
61	100	106	111	116	122	127	132	137	143	148	153	158	164	169	174	180	185
62	104	109	115	120	126	131	136	142	147	153	158	164	169	175	180	186	191
63	107	113	118	124	130	135	141	146	152	158	163	169	175	180	186	191	197
64	110	116	122	128	134	140	145	151	157	163	169	174	180	186	192	197	204
65	114	120	126	132	138	144	150	156	162	168	174	180	186	192	198	204	210
66	118	124	130	136	142	148	155	161	167	173	179	186	192	198	204	210	216
67	121	127	134	140	146	153	159	166	172	178	185	191	198	204	211	217	223
68	125	131	138	144	151	158	164	171	177	184	190	197	203	210	216	223	230
69	128	135	142	149	155	162	169	176	182	189	196	203	209	216	223	230	236
70	132	139	146	153	160	167	174	181	188	195	202	209	216	222	229	236	243
71	136	143	150	157	165	172	179	186	193	200	208	215	222	229	236	243	250
72	140	147	154	162	169	177	184	191	199	206	213	221	228	235	242	250	258
73	144	151	159	166	174	182	189	197	204	212	219	227	235	242	250	257	265
74	148	155	163	171	179	186	194	202	210	218	225	233	241	249	256	264	272
75	152	160	168	176	184	192	200	208	216	224	232	240	248	256	264	272	279
76	156	164	172	180	189	197	205	213	221	230	238	246	254	263	271	279	287

A general formula to determine BMI is as follows: Divide one's weight in kilograms/pounds by height in meters/inches squared. Or another way is to simply multiply weight in pounds by 703, divide by height in inches, then divide again by height in inches. Here's an example. Suppose a person is five feet (60 inches) tall and weighs 120 pounds. Multiply 120 (pounds) by 703, which equals 84,360. Divide that figure by 60 (inches), which equals 1,406. Divide the result again by 60, which equals 23.4, the body mass index. In this case, the BMI is in the normal range.

Source: National Heart, Lung, and Blood Institute, "Body Mass Index Table," n.d., <http://www.nhlbi.nih.gov/guidelines/obesity/bmi_tbl.htm> (June 20, 2005).

teenagers, health care professionals frequently use weight-for-age growth charts, often called BMI-for-age charts. Curved lines on a chart show percentiles, and a person's BMI plotted on the chart indicates whether his or her BMI exceeds or equals the percentage of others of the same age and gender. Suppose a five-year-old girl is in the 50th percentile. This means that 50 percent of girls of the same age have a lower BMI. If a fifteen-year-old boy is in the 60th percentile, this indicates that compared to other boys of the same age, 60 percent have a lower BMI. Whether female or male, youth aged two to twenty are considered overweight if their BMI is in the 95th percentile or higher and underweight if in the 5th percentile or lower.[10]

An Epidemic?

Health officials at the U.S. Department of Health and Human Services (HHS), the U.S. Food and Drug Administration (FDA), the NIH, and other federal agencies have been warning for years that obesity is a growing health problem for the nation and that there is an "obesity epidemic" rampant in the land. Most health care providers and institutions have echoed those alarms.

Yet not everyone agrees. The Center for Consumer Freedom (CCF), which says it "is a nonprofit coalition of restaurants, food companies, and consumers," is a constant critic of what it calls "food cops." CCF believes that people should be able to make their own choices about food, not "health care enforcers" and "meddling bureaucrats" who claim to know what is best for people.[11]

At the same time, some medical experts and researchers emphasize that a healthy lifestyle is more important than trying to reach an ideal body weight. Whether young or old, a person can have excess body fat and still be fit. "Thin people do not have a monopoly on health and fitness. Fit and healthy bodies come in all shapes and sizes," writes Steven N. Blair, director of research at the Cooper Institute for Aerobics Research, in a foreword for the book *Big Fat Lies: The Truth about Your Weight and Your Health*.[12] Blair's research supports "the idea that fitness is more important than fatness," an Associated Press (AP) report notes.[13] He concludes that even though people may be in a high BMI group, they can still be healthy because they are active—they exercise and are not sedentary "couch potatoes." Active people "have lower death rates from all causes—cancer, heart disease, diabetes—than the sedentary and unfit in the normal or lean BMI category," Blair insists.[14] However, he acknowledges that there is "an increasing prevalence of obesity" in the United States, and that there is no doubt that obesity is linked to health problems.[15] But he argues in an editorial in the September 8, 2004, issue of the *JAMA* that too much emphasis is placed on food intake and that more attention should be paid to getting people to exercise. Indeed, two studies published in the same issue of the journal also stress that exercise is an important component in preventing obesity and heart disease.

Paul Campos, a law professor and nationally recognized expert on America's "fat war," also has an opposing view. In his book *The Obesity Myth*, he writes that the panic over obesity is unwarranted. Campos accuses drug companies, medical professionals, diet-food manufacturers, diet gurus, and researchers of perpetuating concerns about obesity. Why? To earn more and more profits for the multi-billion-dollar weight-loss industry.

Another opposing view comes from Dr. Jeffrey Friedman, an obesity researcher at Rockefeller University in New York who discovered leptin, an appetite-suppressing hormone produced by fat cells. From his research, Friedman concludes that like a person's height, body weight is determined by genes, which also control how much a person eats and burns food. In his view, the extent of obesity is being overemphasized in the United States with lots of misinformation circulating. As a

NAME _____

Weight-for-stature percentiles: Boys

RECORD # _____

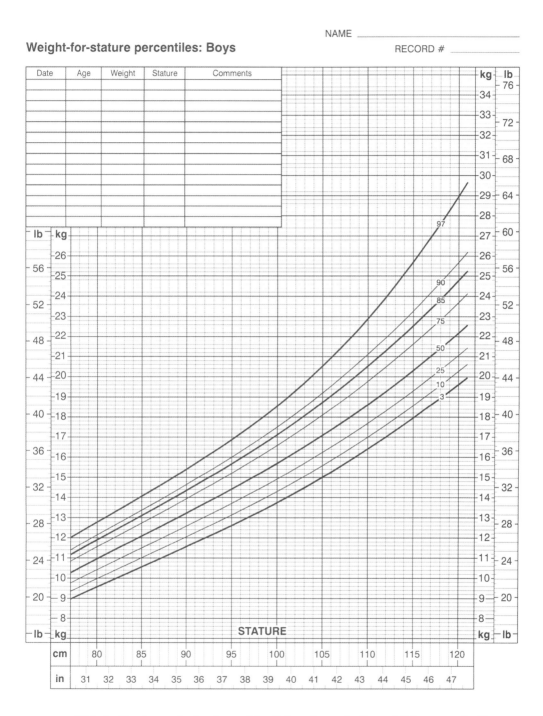

This is the type of chart used to determine whether children are in the right weight range for their age and height.

result, Americans are made to feel guilty if they gain weight. He argues that a careful study of statistics shows that while extremely obese people are increasing in weight, those who are thin are staying about the same; since 1991 Americans on average have gained only seven to ten pounds. "Before calling [obesity] an epidemic, people really need to understand what the numbers do and don't say," he told a *New York Times* reporter.[16]

Debates over whether or not there is an obesity "epidemic" are not likely to fade away. Health experts are focused on the problem, although they acknowledge that the causes of obesity are not yet fully understood. As a result, numerous U.S. agencies and health professionals are continuing to investigate possible factors in the problem of obesity.

Causes of Obesity

Factors that can contribute to being overweight or obese certainly include a person's genes, as Dr. Jeffrey Friedman argues. In fact, many scientists are focusing on the biology of obesity and are now convinced that obesity is a disease. "Increasingly, researchers are demonstrating that obesity is controlled by a powerful biological system of hormones, proteins, neurotransmitters [electrical signals in the brain], and genes that regulate fat storage and body weight and tell the brain when, what, and how much to eat," according to a cover story in *U.S. News & World Report*. The story quotes Louis Aronne, director of the Comprehensive Weight Control Program at New York-Presbyterian Hospital, who says,

"Once people gain weight, then these biological mechanisms, which we're beginning to understand, develop to prevent people from losing weight. It's not someone fighting 'willpower.' The body resists weight loss."[1]

Part of the resistance to weight loss is linked to the fact that humans, like other mammals, have a built-in system that long ago protected them when food was scarce. Their bodies stored fat efficiently. When our ancient ancestors could not obtain sufficient food by hunting for meat and gathering fruits and nuts, they were still able to survive; their bodies used stored fat from food they ate during times of plenty. As humans evolved, they maintained their mechanism to guard against scarcity, but today, with a steady source of food, most Americans do not need to store body fat for survival. In addition, because of labor-saving devices and many modes of transportation, people do not use up body fat. As a result, individuals become overweight and obese.

Health care professionals contend that the major cause of weight gain, overweight, and obesity can be summarized simply: People take in more calories than they burn up in exercise—sports, physical work, and other activities. Calories measure the production of fuel, or energy, produced in the body. When the calories we consume exceed our needs, the "extras" are stored as body fat.

Caloric needs vary with individuals, however. "Average" teenage girls, for example, need only about 2,000 to 2,200 calories daily. "Average" teenage boys may use up to 2,800 calories daily. Teenage athletes or those who are very active, whatever their gender, could have much higher energy needs.

Cultural patterns, economic and social status, and emotional makeup also contribute to weight gain, other experts say. Some people, for example, may eat more than they need because food is comforting—it tastes good and may seem to ease loneliness, loss, sadness, stress, or anxiety. Young people may overeat because they are following a pattern set by their parents and/or their friends. Chronic diseases can also determine whether a person is thin, fat, or in between.

One other factor connected to weight gain and increased BMI may be sleep deprivation—getting only five hours or less of sleep. Some people who are unable to sleep may get up in the middle of the night and snack, thus contributing to weight gain. But according to a long-term, continuing study in which more than one thousand volunteers have been participating, researchers found that lack of sleep affects the levels of two hormones that control appetite: leptin and ghrelin. Leptin suppresses appetite and ghrelin stimulates appetite.

Participants in the study who did not get enough sleep had low levels of leptin and elevated ghrelin—16 percent less leptin and nearly 15 percent more ghrelin than those who regularly slept seven to eight hours. In Western societies like the United States where people commonly have restricted sleep patterns and food is readily available, changes in the hormones that regulate appetite "may contribute to obesity," the study concludes.[2]

> Part of the resistance to weight loss is linked to the fact that humans, like other mammals, have a built-in system that long ago protected them when food was scarce. Their bodies store fat efficiently.

Lack of Exercise

Lack of exercise plays a major role in weight gain, experts say, and some health professionals insist that inactivity is the leading cause of obesity in young people. Two medical studies published in 2004 found that when overweight and obese children and teenagers engaged in vigorous exercise, they not only lost weight but also reversed damage to their arteries—damage that could lead to heart attack or stroke.

In one of the studies by researchers in San Diego, California, 878 adolescents aged eleven to fifteen took part. For a year the young people kept track of their diet and physical activities. When researchers analyzed the data, they found that "insufficient vigorous physical activity," was the main risk factor for adolescent boys and girls to develop a high BMI.[3] As Kevin Patrick, M.D., who led the study, explained further, "Too much time spent . . . at computer games and watching TV may equal, or even exceed, diet . . . as important contributors to overweight in adolescence."[4]

In other studies, data from the CDC, FDA, and other federal agencies gathered from 1980 to 2000 show that physical activity fell sharply among students twelve to nineteen years of age. In 1980, 42 percent of teens surveyed were physically active but in 2000 only 29 percent of teenagers said they engaged in some sort of physical activity for at least thirty minutes a day. During that same twenty-year period, teenage obesity increased by 10 percent. "Nearly half of American youths aged 12–21 years are not vigorously active on a regular basis," according to the HHS. "About 14 percent of young people report no recent physical activity." More female than male young people are inactive—14 percent of females compared to 7 percent of males.[5] HHS studies have found a striking decline in physical activity as a young person's age or grade in school increases.

The reasons for inactivity are many. In some cases, families do not use available sports or recreational facilities and playgrounds in their communities because of safety concerns—fears about drug use, violence, bullying, or other threats. Or perhaps there are no parks, walkways, or bicycle trails nearby.

Many U.S. families live in sprawling suburban communities where stores and other businesses are not within walking distance. People usually drive to get to their destinations, which contributes to an inactive lifestyle.

Whatever the distance from home to school, U.S. teenagers are likely to drive and younger students are usually driven to school and other activities. Even though a majority of students live within a mile of their school, only 28 percent of them go there on foot. Only 17 percent of all students walk to school, according to a *Time* magazine report.[6]

Another factor leading to inactivity is the growing number of students who avoid physical education (P.E.) or have little chance to take part in class exercises. In many elementary schools, P.E. may be offered only once or twice per week. Nationwide, in 2003 only 28 percent of high school students took part in daily P.E. classes, according to the CDC.[7]

In some states, school gym classes have been cut because of reductions in staff and funding. Consider Michigan. About one fourth of sixth grade students in the state have no P.E. classes for the entire year and two thirds of high school students do not participate in a P.E. class or do not take part because gym classes are not available. Yet the Governor's Council on Physical Fitness, Health and Sports believes that "cutting gym to balance budgets is the wrong approach." The chair of the council, Charles Kuntzleman, a University of Michigan professor, says the state is "either going to pay now or later, and now is going to be a lot cheaper than later," when health costs due to over-weight and obesity may be much higher than the cost of gym classes.[8]

As Dr. Patrick of San Diego concluded, watching television and playing video or computer games are other reasons young people (and adults) do not exercise. Kelly D. Brownell, a Yale University expert on eating disorders and obesity, cites study after study "showing that TV time is coupled with both obesity and poor food consumption in children and adults, males and females, and people across countries." By the time U.S. students graduate from high school, they "have accumulated more hours before the TV than in school, and this must be added to the hours people spend with video games and computers," Dr. Brownell writes.[9]

Studies show that teens who exercise regularly are less likely to be overweight. However, activity levels have fallen in recent years among young people.

Abundant Food Supply

While an inactive lifestyle and high-calorie snacks and meals get a lot of blame for weight problems, some researchers point to the nation's food system as another contributor, directly or indirectly, to America's reputation as *Fat Land* (the title of Greg Critser's book on the subject). Over the past few decades, the food supply, the kinds of food, and the way people eat have changed considerably.

One major change can be seen in agriculture and the manufacture of food products in the United States. Even though many people believe that much of the American food supply comes from family farms of the "Old MacDonald" variety, that type of small family farm and family farms in general have been disappearing. Since about the 1950s, food production for the most part has become industrialized. Vast corporate-owned farmlands specialize in growing one type of crop or produce, or they concentrate on giant livestock operations (sometimes called "factory farms") that generate great quantities of meat or poultry.

"The greater efficiency, specialization, and size of agriculture and food product manufacture have led to one of the great unspoken secrets about the American food system: overabundance," writes Marion Nestle, professor and chair of the Department of Nutrition, Food Studies and Public Health at New York University.[10]

Government subsidies have also contributed to the plentiful supply of processed foods. The federal government pays some farmers to raise such crops as corn, wheat, rice, soybeans, and sugar, prompting increased production and ever more food products high in calories. The relatively low cost of these foods creates intense competition among processors. Rather than raise prices to increase profits on competing items, manufacturers compete by introducing thousands of new processed food products each year. "More than two-thirds of those products are condiments, candy and snacks, baked goods, soft drinks, and dairy products," Nestle writes.[11] Many of these items are high in calories and low in nutritional value, putting them in the category that dieticians and others label as junk food (which includes beverages).

To sell junk food, companies aim a major portion of their advertising toward young people. The marketing begins with ads directed at toddlers and preschoolers. On youngsters' TV programs, commercials peddle such products as sugary foods and soft drinks. Children who watch these programs are likely to see a food commercial every five minutes. One U.S. study that examined food advertising on children's TV found:

> On average, 11 of 19 commercials per hour were for food. Of [564] ads, 246 (44%) promoted food from the fats and sweets group, such as candy, soft drinks, chips, cakes, cookies and pastries. . . . The most frequently advertised food product was high sugar breakfast cereal.

Many food and soft drink TV commercials as well as print ads are also aimed at adolescents. "Food marketers are interested in youth as consumers because of their spending power, their purchasing influence, and as future adult consumers," the researchers note.[12]

Whatever the targets, advertising costs the food and beverage industry huge sums. Pepsi, for example, "spends an estimated $2.1 billion a year on marketing, McDonald's $1.2 billion, and Coca-Cola is not far behind at $895 million," according to the Washington State Department of Health. While much marketing takes place on television, magazine and store ads also tout junk food, as do movies in which products are strategically placed. Does all this advertising work? Apparently, since "Americans spent $110 billion on fast food in 2001 and consumed 56 gallons of soda per person" or almost six hundred 12-ounce cans.[13]

The Fast-Food Connection

Excess calories also come from convenience foods sold in stores and meals served at family and fast-food restaurants. Large-size frozen meals and packaged items such as macaroni and cheese in supermarkets, buckets (rather than small containers) of buttered popcorn at the movies, and super-sized soft drinks and sandwiches at fast-food establishments are common.

It is true that some fast-food companies have started to serve smaller portions and lower calorie meals—McDonald's salads and adult Happy Meals with salad, bottled water, and a pedometer to encourage walking are examples. Other chains such as Wendy's and Burger King are also offering nutritious items such as milk or fruit juice that can be selected instead of sugary soft drinks; fruit cups and salads can be chosen rather than high-calorie, high-fat fries. Some chain restaurants offer sandwiches or pizzas that are lower in fat than their regular varieties. Nevertheless, there are still numerous choices for foods and beverages that can add to weight problems.

Yet that does not mean that most teenagers worry about fast-food consumption. It is not unusual to hear teenagers say that they do not care about calories in colas or hamburgers and fries. They choose these items because they taste good, not because they worry about what is good for them.

Fast foods such as burgers and fries are an easy place to find extra calories.

A study of 6,200 U.S. children and teenagers aged four to nineteen, published in January 2004 in *Pediatrics,* found that on any typical day about one third (30.3 percent) ate fast food.[14] Another study of teens aged thirteen to fifteen in fifteen industrialized countries concludes that "U.S. teens were more likely than those in other countries to eat fast food, snacks and sugary sodas." This fact, claim the authors of the study, published in the *Archives of Pediatrics & Adolescent Medicine,* contributes to the rate of obesity among U.S. teens that is higher than the rate in fourteen other countries. However, Greece, Portugal, Israel, Ireland, and Denmark are not far behind the United States. Of the fifteen countries in the study, the rates for obesity and overweight are the lowest for teens in Lithuania, perhaps because there are not as many fast-food restaurants in Lithuania and teens do not have as much money to spend on snacks and fast food as their counterparts in other industrialized nations, one of the authors of the study reports.[15]

A different kind of study conducted by researchers at Children's Hospital in Boston, Massachusetts, focused on teens thirteen to seventeen years old who regularly eat at fast-food restaurants. Fifty-four teenagers in the first part of the study were taken to a fast-food court and allowed to eat whatever they wanted. Secondly, researchers allowed the same group of teenagers to go to a fast-food restaurant of their choice: Burger King, KFC, McDonald's, Taco Bell, or Wendy's. "The participants were required to get one item with protein plus a side item, such as French fries or a soda," according to a news report. What did the researchers learn? On average, the teenagers consumed over fifteen hundred calories in fast food—more than half of their daily needs—but to offset the high calories, slim teenagers ate less later in the day, while overweight teens did not adjust their food intake and added about four hundred more calories to their daily fare.[16]

School Vending Machines

One more guilty party in the problem of overweight students may be the school vending machine, say many nutrition experts and government officials. In 2000, the CDC found that 43 percent of elementary schools, 89.4 percent of middle/junior high schools, and 98.2 percent of senior high schools had either a vending machine or a school store, canteen, or snack bar. At the machines or stores, students could buy foods or beverages other than what was offered by school lunch programs.[17]

To determine what vending machines offer for sale, the Center for Science in the Public Interest (CSPI) conducted a nationwide survey in 2003 of more than fourteen hundred vending machines in 251 middle schools and high schools. The CSPI found that 75 percent of drinks and 85 percent of snacks in the machines were of poor nutritional quality and usually high in calories. Common items were soda, imitation fruit juices, candy, chips, cookies, and snack cakes. With so much junk food in school vending machines, there is little incentive for students to make healthy food choices.[18]

In the words of Senator Tom Harkin of Iowa, "Junk foods in school vending machines compete with, and ultimately undermine, the nutritious meals offered by the federal school lunch program." According to Harkin, "Congress should step in and ensure that soda, candy, chips, and cookies don't become the de facto [actual] school lunch." He would like the U.S. Department of Agriculture (USDA) "to set standards for all foods sold in schools that participate in the federal school lunch program."[19]

Schools across the United States have been considering bans on or have restricted access to vending machines that offer junk food and sugary soft drinks. Some individual schools have removed sodas and candy from their vending machines. In some states, students are limited to using vending machines and canteens at certain times during the school day. Other states require that at least half of all foods and drinks offered in vending machines in each school district include healthful items, such as granola bars, fresh fruit, 100 percent fruit juices, bottled water, and milk.

While restrictions are more widely accepted today than a few years ago, outright bans on vending machines are controversial. Many teenagers, for example, believe they should be able to make their own choices about what they will eat and drink.

Arguments for vending machines also come from some school administrators and school boards who want to earn funds for their schools. How is that done? Soft-drink companies and other vendors provide beverages and snacks, and schools earn a percentage of the profits from product sales—particularly soft drinks, which may also be advertised in schools. A school, for example, may get a scoreboard, T-shirts, or other items adorned with brand names or product decals. The money from vending machine sales pays for sports programs and equipment, band uniforms, computers, and other "extras" that school administrators say they cannot afford because of cutbacks in tax funds allocated for schools. Some individual schools have earned as much as $100,000 each year.[20] Urban districts with many schools take in much more. For example, the Seattle, Washington, school district earns about $330,000 annually from vending machine sales.[21]

Some experts contend that vending machines may not be the culprits they are made out to be. They believe schools should promote weight loss with physical education and encourage healthy diets through nutrition classes. Others argue that beyond school classes, many more educational programs are needed to help the public understand the importance of nutrition and eating healthy foods, and what the health risks are for people who are overweight or obese.

3　Health Risks and Costs

Government agencies and health professionals who gather statistics and distribute information on obesity often emphasize the health risks for those who are obese. According to the NIH, diseases and health problems linked to obesity include diabetes; cardiovascular problems (heart disease, stroke, and damaged blood vessels); gallbladder disease and gallstones; liver disease; osteoarthritis (a deterioration of the joints sometimes due to excess weight); gout (a disease that affects joints); pulmonary (breathing) problems, including sleep apnea, in which a person can stop breathing for a short time during sleep; and reproductive problems in women, including menstrual irregularities and infertility.

Obesity is also linked to various cancers. Obese men are more likely than men who maintain a healthy weight to die from cancer of the colon, rectum, or prostate. Obese women are more likely than those who are not obese to die from cancer of the gallbladder, breast, uterus, cervix, or ovaries.[1]

Diabetes and Obesity

The link between diabetes and obesity is of special concern, especially as an increasing number of overweight young people are diagnosed with the disease. An estimated 13 million Americans have diabetes, and another 5 million or more may have the disease but do not know it, according to the American Diabetes Association (ADA).[2]

Diabetes is a disease in which the body does not produce or properly use insulin, a hormone that converts glucose (sugar) and starches (like potatoes) into the energy that body cells need to function. There are two kinds of diabetes, Type I and Type II. Type I, once called juvenile diabetes, is usually diagnosed in children and young adults—their bodies do not produce insulin and they need several insulin injections a day or an insulin pump to survive.

About 90 percent of diabetics have Type II, and their symptoms may appear slowly as their bodies, for various reasons, fail to produce enough insulin or to use insulin efficiently. Type II diabetes was once an adult disease, but it has been rising steadily in all children, especially African-American, Hispanic, and American Indian adolescents, according to reports from clinics around the country. "What was once a disease of our grandparents is now a disease of our children," says Dr. Francine Kaufman, director of the Comprehensive Childhood Diabetes Center at the Childrens Hospital Los Angeles.[3] Because this is a relatively new trend, there are no accurate statistics on children and adolescents who have Type

II diabetes. But the ADA does note, "As many as 80 percent of [diabetic] youth may be overweight at the time of diagnosis."[4]

One teenager with Type II diabetes is fourteen-year-old Jalisa Young of St. Petersburg, Florida, who was featured in a special report published in the *St. Petersburg Times*. Jalisa has a family history of diabetes and is overweight. She was diagnosed with diabetes in 2002, when she was twelve years old, but at first she "wasn't really paying attention," she told a reporter. "I was ready to go back to playing and stuff, with my friends."[5] And she continued to eat sugary snacks like candy and plenty of French fries.

Then Jalisa's doctor told her that she could suffer serious complications that could not be reversed. She needed to take care of herself: eat properly, take her medication to increase her insulin, and exercise. High levels of sugar in the cells can lead to such problems as damage to blood vessels and nerves in the legs and feet (requiring amputations) and blindness. Today, Jalisa is careful about her diet, substituting healthy snacks like sunflower seeds for candy. She also exercises by riding her bike and walking. Yet, it is not easy for teens (or adults for that matter) to adjust to being diabetic. As Jalisa put it, "You miss out on a lot of stuff."[6]

Health problems that have been linked to obesity include diabetes, cardiovascular disease, gallbladder disease and gallstones, liver disease, osteoarthritis, and breathing disorders.

In 2004, the National Institute of Diabetes and Digestive and Kidney Diseases of the NIH began a study, enrolling 750 young people aged ten to seventeen with Type II diabetes. The purpose of the five-year study is to evaluate treatments so that doctors can effectively help young patients. Participants are assigned to three treatment groups. One group takes a medication called metformin that reduces the amount of glucose the liver makes; the second group uses a combination of metformin and another drug, rosiglitazone, which helps muscle cells respond to insulin and use glucose more efficiently; and the third group takes metformin and is also part of a regimen for losing weight and increasing physical activity. Along with studying how each treatment approach controls blood glucose levels, the trial will evaluate the costs of treatment and the health risks diabetic youth face.

Metabolic Syndrome and Obesity

Nearly one million adolescents in the United States are affected by metabolic syndrome, a medical term for a set of characteristics that can lead to the early onset of diabetes and also heart disease. Researchers at the University of Rochester (New York) say that a young person who has at least three out of five of the following characteristics is at risk:

- high blood pressure
- high triglycerides (blood fats that increase the risk of heart disease)
- low HDL-cholesterol (HDL stands for high-density lipoproteins, which carry away the fatlike substance known as cholesterol)
- high blood sugar that can lead to diabetes
- abdominal obesity (fat around the waist)

The researchers reviewed data on 2,430 adolescents aged twelve to nineteen and concluded that at least 4 percent of all U.S. adolescents and 30 percent of all overweight adolescents met the criteria for metabolic syndrome. Michael Weitzman, M.D., professor of pediatrics at Rochester University, points out, "With this new information, when doctors see adolescent patients who are overweight, they will know to look for signs of metabolic syndrome, and to aggressively work with the patient to promote a healthier diet and lifestyle."[7]

Ethnicity and Risk

The burden of overweight and obesity is not evenly distributed across ethnic groups in the United States, and federal agencies try to determine which American groups are at risk for health problems linked to a high BMI. Groups are categorized by age, gender, race, cultural background, income, social status, and geographic locations. This is *not* an effort to humiliate people or discriminate against particular groups. Rather, it is one way to build awareness and encourage action to prevent obesity and the increased health risks associated with it.

For example, major findings from a federal survey in 2003 indicate that 30 percent of non-Hispanic white women are obese, 40 percent of Mexican-American women are obese, and 51 percent of non-Hispanic African-American women are obese, according to a FDA spokesperson. In addition, death rates from diseases often associated with obesity are higher for the African-American population than for the white population: 40 percent more from stroke, 29 percent more from heart disease, and 25 percent more from cancer.[8]

Young people of Mexican heritage and non-Hispanic African Americans are also more likely to be overweight and obese than non-Hispanic whites. The CDC reports that among young people aged twelve to nineteen, 27.5 percent of Mexican-American boys and 19.4 percent of Mexican-American girls are overweight. Among non-Hispanic African Americans, the figures are 20.7 percent for boys and 26.6 percent for girls. For non-Hispanic whites, 12.8 percent of boys and 12.4 percent of girls are considered overweight.[9]

Obesity is also more likely in the Southeast region of the United States than in other parts of the nation. "All Southeastern states except Florida have higher rates than the national average," reports the AARP (formerly known as the American Association of Retired Persons), which advocates for older Americans. This means that each year in the Southeast $13 billion is spent on obesity-related medical conditions—"a dangerous drain on funding for other health concerns."[10]

Poverty and Obesity

Money—or lack of it—can determine whether a population group is at risk for obesity and associated health problems. In the United States and some other industrialized nations, poverty and obesity often coexist. Although low income does not necessarily indicate that members of a family will have unhealthy diets or tend to be fat, numerous studies have shown that impoverished people are more likely to be obese than those of higher economic status.

A 2002 study by the *American Journal of Clinical Nutrition* reported that low-income women are 50 percent more likely to be obese than affluent women. Why? Part of the reason is that the foods a family can afford are those that are filling but high in calories. Nutritious, low-calorie foods like fresh fruits and vegetables, fish, and lean meat cost more than, say, a pizza or candy bar that eases hunger and provides quick energy but is high in calories. As writer Bethany Spicher asks in *Sojourners Magazine*, "If you were hungry, would you spend your last food dollar on energy-packed pasta or nutrient-rich greens?"[11]

Another reason for the link between poverty and obesity is that poor families often have limited access to nutritious foods or have little choice in the selection of foods in grocery stores. This is especially true in inner-city neighborhoods where there are few if any nearby supermarkets. "The wealthiest neighborhoods have more than three times as many supermarkets as the poorest ones" and "the gap is even wider along racial lines, with white neighborhoods having as many as four times the number of supermarkets as black ones," writes Tracie McMillan in *City Limits.*[12]

Low-income residents frequently have to use public transportation to find a major grocery store, and returning on a bus or subway with bags of groceries can be extremely difficult. So the

Exercise and a nutritious diet can help young people avoid the health risks associated with obesity.

alternative in inner-city areas may be to shop at a neighborhood store or eat at a nearby fast-food restaurant that offers large portions for a low price.

Mari Gallagher of the Metropolitan Chicago Information Center explains,

> In most poor neighborhoods, there are plenty of storefronts, where you can buy a box of Pampers, a pack of cigarettes and a can of Campbell's soup. But you just can't get a full range of healthy products like fruits and vegetables and 2 percent milk. Many of these neighborhood grocers are really just glorified liquor stores.[13]

In many U.S. rural areas, families may have access to grocery stores, but poverty often prevents them from developing healthy eating habits. Consider southeastern Ohio, which has higher than average rates of both obesity and poverty. In the rural area around Marietta, Ohio, low income has definitely been linked to obesity, but health officials say lifestyle choices are also to blame. "That includes eating fast food, watching too much television and failing to participate in exercise programs" in schools (which have been cut due to lack of funds), a news report states.[14]

Measuring Costs

Along with all the studies and national data collected on people at risk, the costs of obesity are tabulated as well. These costs include medical expenses to treat problems that are linked to obesity. Illness and disease are the worst part of the obesity problem, but economic costs accentuate the hardship. Direct U.S. health costs due to obesity in 2003 totaled $75 billion, according to the CDC. At the state level, the costs range from $87 million in Wyoming to $7.7 billion in California.[15] When the costs of obesity-associated health care and lost work time due to illness are added together, the total is estimated at $117 billion a year, says a spokesman for the FDA.[16]

For youth aged six to seventeen, hospital costs for obesity-related diseases tripled from 1979 to 1999, the most recent year for such data. In addition, the length of the hospital stays increased from almost a week to almost two weeks.[17]

In the opinion of former HHS Secretary Tommy Thompson, lack of physical activity is a major contributor to overweight among youths and the medical costs that are likely to accompany obesity. Whether young people will get more active in order to maintain good health and avoid medical costs is a big question mark at this time. But it is certain that a great many adolescents believe that they are "too fat," and in their view not acceptable among their peers. So teens try dieting to lose weight or they wonder if weight-loss diets are for them.

What About Weight-Loss Diets?

Negative Calorie Diet. Sun Slim Diet. Ten Day Easy Diet. Slimfast Jumpstart Diet. Scarsdale Low-Carb Diet. Zone Diet. South Beach Diet. Atkins Diet. Sexy People Diet. Cabbage Soup Diet. Grapefruit Diet.

Chances are you have seen advertisements for diets like these just listed. There are hundreds of them. They are frequently called "fad diets," which the University of Pittsburgh (Pennsylvania) Medical Center defines as an eating plan that

promises quick weight loss through what is usually an unhealthy and unbalanced diet. Fad diets are targeted at people who want to lose weight quickly without exercise. Some fad diets claim that they make you lose fat, but it's really water weight you're losing. Fad diets that are restricted to certain foods may work, but most are boring or unappealing. This can make them difficult to follow on a long-term basis. And some fad diets can actually be harmful to your health.[1]

To control their weight, millions of people look for "quick fix" solutions such as all-liquid diets (which in most cases pose dangerous health risks) or diets that focus on eating a specific food. Consider the Cabbage Soup Diet or the Grapefruit Diet. Eating just one type of food in unlimited amounts while eliminating items in other food groups is not nutritionally sound. Cabbage soup can be a healthy meal, but consuming it for most meals can cause gas and bloating. Grapefruit may help curb appetite before a meal or it can be a nutritious snack, but it has no special qualities to burn off fat.

Teens at Risk

Claims about the effectiveness of fad diets seem to be everywhere: on television, billboards, the Internet, and in magazines, newspapers, and flyers. With all the recent focus on the dangers of obesity, teens may believe they should diet to lose weight. Many may try a highly advertised and popular eating plan. In fact, "Eighty percent of the teenage girls in the United States have been on at least one diet," writes Glenn Gaesser, a University of Virginia professor.[2]

Any type of fad diet can put teenagers at risk, preventing them from getting the nutrients they need for healthy growth, experts insist. The American Academy of Family Physicians provides some general cues on how to recognize fad diets, warning that you should stay away from diets or products if they

• Claim to help you lose weight very quickly (more than one or two pounds per week).

- Promise that you can lose weight and keep it off without giving up "fatty" foods or exercising on a regular basis.

- Base claims on "before and after" photos or offer testimonials from clients or "experts" who are probably being paid to advertise the diet plan or product.

- Draw simple conclusions from complex medical research.

- Limit your food choices and do not encourage you to get balanced nutrition by eating a variety of foods.

- Require you to spend a lot of money on things like seminars, pills, or prepackaged meals in order for the plan to work.[3]

Many teens access the Internet for advice, but the safest course is to turn to the family doctor, a nurse, or a reputable nutritionist. Some questions a teenager or adult might ask are likely to focus on the popular low-carbohydrate (low-carb) and high-protein diets and foods in supermarkets and restaurants. What are carbohydrates and proteins? They are nutrients that the body needs along with fat and vitamins and minerals. Carbs are the body's principal sources of energy and are found in starches (grains, rice, pasta, potatoes), most fruits, and sugars. Protein is the basic substance of every cell in the body and is found in such foods as meat, poultry, fish, dairy products, and legumes.

Low-Carb Diets

Restricting the intake of carbohydrates is the basis for not only the Atkins Diet but also for the High Protein Diet, Hollywood Diet, Protein Power, South Beach Diet, and the Zone Diet, among others. These diets were developed in recent times, but long before they became popular William Banting, a carpenter and undertaker in England, wrote a booklet in the mid-1800s advocating a high-protein, low-carb diet—a plan that he followed to lose weight. Since that time, developers of these plans claim that when a person eats foods low in carbs, the body automatically will burn more fat for energy and thus promote weight loss.

The Atkins Diet is the most widely used low-carb diet today. It is named for the late Robert C. Atkins, M.D., who published his *Diet Revolution* in 1972 and the *New Diet Revolution* twenty years later. Both books have sold millions of copies, and thousands of dieters claim success with the Atkins plan.

Any type of fad diet can put teens at risk, preventing them from getting the nutrients they need for healthy growth.

To "do Atkins," as the books and dieters refer to it, people severely limit high-carb foods—breads, pasta, fruits, sugar, and some vegetables. But the diet allows people to eat unlimited amounts of protein-rich foods and fat-laced foods such as butter, cheese, and mayonnaise.

However, the diet has been controversial ever since it was first initiated. Some health experts consider the diet dangerous because it limits carbohydrates the body needs and allows many protein foods that are high in fat content. High-fat diets can increase the risk for heart disease and obesity.

One group that formed in 2004 and is especially critical of Atkins and other low-carb diets is the Partnership for Essential Nutrition (PEN). It includes nonprofit organizations such as the American Association of Diabetes Educators, American Institute for Cancer Research, American Obesity Association, National Consumers League, National Women's Health Resource Center, University of California at Davis, and Yale-Griffin Prevention Research Center. The coalition explains the theory that is the basis for low-carb plans. These diets

> force the body to use fat as its main energy source, resulting in "ketosis," a process that is jump-started by eliminating carbohydrates, and specifically glucose, which is what the brain needs for normal functioning. When faced with no dietary carbohydrates,

the brain first causes the body to metabolize [change and use] the stores of carbohydrates in the liver and in the muscles and then to metabolize protein in the muscles, which can be converted to carbohydrates. With continued [reduction of] carbohydrate[s], the body converts to using fat and the brain is forced to use the metabolic breakdown products of fat, called "ketones," as the source of energy.[4]

As this process begins, ketones are released in urine and dieters lose water, which usually results in weight loss. But as some dieters and health experts point out, lost water may be regained (along with weight) when people resume their customary eating routine. And many people do discontinue diet plans like Atkins because they are difficult, restrictive, and often expensive to maintain (Atkins, for example, requires dieters to take a host of vitamin and mineral supplements).

Controversy surrounding the low-carb Atkins diet plan has prompted medical studies to determine if its claims are valid. In 2003, for instance, an issue of the *New England Journal of Medicine* included studies that compared the amount of weight lost by severely obese individuals on the Atkins diet with weight lost by people following a more conventional low-fat, low-calorie diet. Researchers found that Atkins dieters lost weight more quickly than the other group, but by the end of a year there were no differences in weight loss. These studies concluded that in the short term, low-carb diets can result in rapid weight loss (up to twenty pounds in a few weeks), but there is not yet evidence that such diets are effective or safe over the long term. Safety concerns regarding low-carb diets are related to whether eating high-fat foods for more than a year will result in risks for heart disease, stroke, or other health problems.

In an ABC News interview, Dr. Robert Eckel, professor of medicine at the University of Colorado Health Science Center in Denver, was asked whether he would advise following the

Low-carb diets can be short on important nutrients, such as the whole grains contained in this sandwich.

Atkins diet for six months and then switching to a more conventional diet. His response:

> No, I would not recommend using the Atkins diet even for short periods . . . I think we need to teach good lifestyle habits that are more likely to be effective and safe long term. People need to realize that rapid weight loss is often not sustained.[5]

Nevertheless, some doctors recommend using modified

versions of low-carb, high-protein diets (such as the South Beach Diet); they also advise eating more fish and chicken rather than pork and beef. "Low-carb diets may be an important weight control option for many obese, or severely obese patients," according to Dr. Howard Eisenson, who heads the Duke University Diet and Fitness Center.[6]

Diet Programs

Some diet programs do make an effort to encourage a variety of choices. Two examples are Weight Watchers and the Jenny Craig Diet Program. There are few if any forbidden foods, but dieters are expected to limit the caloric content of their meals. For example, Weight Watchers, which has millions of followers worldwide, uses a point system to help dieters determine their calorie count. Both programs have support systems: Participants in Weight Watchers attend classes and meetings with other dieters; Jenny Craig dieters meet with a counselor once a week.

Drawbacks to these programs include the expenses for membership fees and meetings. For Jenny Craig dieters there are additional costs for prepared meals and vitamin and mineral supplements that they are advised to take. If dieters leave a program, there is another downside: They may be dependent on others to maintain a healthy eating pattern and fail to continue on their own without others' support or printed guidelines.

Although some overweight young people have tried Weight Watchers (usually because parents have advocated it), the program announced in 2003 that those aged ten to sixteen must have a doctor's referral and the signature of a parent or guardian to become a member. The program does not accept children under age ten. Limiting access to children came about after "a thorough investigation into the state of the science in this area and found it to be almost uniformly disappointing." According to Karen Miller Kovach, chief scientist and global director of the program, "The methods deemed most appropriate for adults cannot simply be assumed to be appropriate for all children." She adds, "I challenge anyone who currently says that they have a safe and effective weight-loss program for children to back up their claims with long-term data."[7]

Healthy Eating

"Get away from the mentality of a diet" and put the emphasis "on healthy eating and lifestyle changes," says Bettye Nowlin, a dietician with the American Dietetic Association.[8] Marilyn Tanner, another dietician, takes a similar view and underscores the importance of regular exercise in her program for overweight teens at St. Louis (Missouri) Children's Hospital. She points out that the program sets goals that teens can achieve, such as more activity. "The kids wear pedometers," she says. "We find out what their baseline steps are [each day] and add 100 steps or more." While enrolled in the ten-week program, teens learn about nutrition and the importance of eating five servings of fruits and vegetables, limiting fat, and setting a daily goal for calories (such as 2,000). Tanner explains, "Some kids drink the equivalent of 1,000 calories a day in soda." While not all teens lose weight on the program, the main idea is to first establish healthy habits and then work on weight loss. The hope is that teens will then have the tools to control their weight for the rest of their life.[9]

Yet controlling one's weight in early adolescence does not mean pushing the panic button if there are sudden increases in body fat. Dieticians, nutritionists, and doctors stress that children's growth and development may happen in spurts. Before puberty, children gain some fat as part of the normal growth process. In early adolescence some may appear "chubby" for a time, but after they grow a few inches, their weight is appropriate for their age and gender.

In addition, the experts point out that whatever a person's

The New Food Pyramid

The U.S. Department of Agriculture (USDA) recently unveiled its new food pyramid—now called an interactive food guidance system—to help people make healthy decisions about what to eat. The pyramid shows the approximate proportions that should be eaten from the different food groups—grains, vegetables, fruits, milk, and meat and beans. People can get personal dietary recommendations based on their age, gender, and level of activity from the USDA Web site.

MyPyramid
STEPS TO A HEALTHIER YOU
MyPyramid.gov

GRAINS   VEGETABLES   FRUITS   MILK   MEAT & BEANS

age, it is important to be active and eat foods as recommended in the federal government's 2005 Dietary Guidelines for Americans, and the food guidance system, which is a revised version of the familiar USDA food pyramid created in 1992.

The guidelines encourage Americans to eat foods and drink beverages with less sugar and fewer calories. Young children who are already somewhat overweight especially need to limit sugary drinks, even fruit juice; whole fresh fruits are better, say government researchers. Indeed, a study of 10,904 children published in *Pediatrics* underscores this advice. CDC researchers looked at three groups of Missouri preschoolers: those who were in the normal or underweight categories on growth charts; those at risk of becoming overweight (in the 85th to the 95th percentiles); and those who were already overweight. The study found that three and four year olds in the 85th to 95th percentile who consumed one to three sweet drinks (including juice) each day were likely to be seriously overweight a year later. Yet those youngsters below the 85th percentile were not significantly affected by consuming sweet drinks. The researchers point out, "Additional studies are needed to understand better the mechanism by which this consumption [of sweet drinks] contributes to overweight."[10]

For all ages, other key recommendations in the federal government guidelines include increasing consumption of fresh fruit as well as vegetables, whole grains, and fat-free or low-fat milk and dairy products like cheese. Keep total fat intake between 25 to 35 percent of calories for children and adolescents four to eighteen years of age, the guidelines advise. Most fats should come from sources such as fish, nuts, and vegetable oils.

The guidelines also stress the importance of exercise, suggesting that children and adolescents engage in at least sixty minutes of physical activity every day, if possible, or at least most days of the week. Not only does regular physical activity help reduce weight but it also decreases risk factors for cardiovascular and other chronic diseases and improves a person's self-esteem and self-concept.

More Diet Dangers

In late 2003, Kevin Zhou, then a sophomore at Monte Vista High School in Danville, California, posted an article on *Online NewsHour* about the way the media cover teen obesity. In his view, the media have become almost obsessed with the story of obese teens and overlook "the dangers of teens who will do anything to stay slim." He points out, "Pop culture has taught us that being skinny is good, and that being overweight is not. Students know that putting on too many pounds may put their social status in jeopardy." Zhou worried that the emphasis on the threat of obesity will cause those with "a solvable weight problem to turn to life-threatening ways of losing the extra weight."

Zhou is aware of the health risks of being obese, but he believes that "if news organizations want to report on teenage obesity, they should take up the responsibility of providing both sides of the issue and discuss anorexia and bulimia as well."[1]

The eating disorders Zhou mentions—anorexia nervosa and bulimia nervosa—are serious problems that can develop among young people who may not be overweight or obese but think they are. Victims of anorexia have an intense fear of gaining weight and starve themselves, while people with bulimia eat but purge themselves of food by forced vomiting or by the excess use of laxatives. Both anorexics and bulimics place an abnormal emphasis on weight and body image and are usually secretive about their rituals. The disorders can have damaging health effects that can be long lasting and even lead to death.

Of course, most people who struggle to lose weight will not develop an eating disorder. But the continual blitz of media images that idealize being thin can trigger some risky behavior among those who think they are "too heavy" but in reality are an appropriate weight for their height, age, and gender.

Diet Pills, Supplements, and Injections

Fad dieting, as already discussed, is just one of the dangers facing those who are eager to be thin. Health risks may also come in the form of diet pills and dietary supplements, which include weight-loss products as well as vitamins and minerals and products that claim to treat everything from allergies to stress.

Sales pitches for diet pills and potions carry such descriptions as "miracle diet pills," "herbal slimming pills," "weight-loss supplements," "fat-burner diet pills," "diet teas," "appetite suppressants," and "natural diet pills." Such terms frequently imply an almost magical method for losing weight, and they are widely used in advertising to generate annual sales in the billions of dollars. In fact, diet pills and supplements are expected to generate at least $3.5 billion in 2006. Add to that such products as diet soft drinks, diet books and videos, health club revenues, low-calorie diet foods, and other items, and the estimated total income for the diet industry for 2006 reaches $49 billion, according to a news report.[2]

In 2004, the TV program *20/20* reported on its investigation of diet pill ads and found that "misleading tactics" were used to promote the effectiveness of some products. Sometimes before-and-after photographs of people who provide testimonials for diet pills are manipulated or just plain phony. For example, a person paid to do a commercial might be told to gain weight and be photographed for a "before" picture and then take pills and work out to show weight loss in an "after" picture. One of the most serious allegations in the *20/20* program focused on the validity of medical claims. Some doctors are paid to promote a product in commercials but do not actually advise their patients to use it. The program concluded with these words of advice: "The bottom line: Never underestimate how low some marketers will go to sell you that magic pill. Just remember, the only real magic is diet, exercise and a healthy dose of skepticism."[3]

One of the latest weight-loss fads is mesotherapy, a procedure that involves hundreds of injections under the skin. The mixture injected consists of medications, extracts from plants, and vitamins. Supposedly these injections help a person shed fat in waste products.

Singer Roberta Flack, with her endorsement, helped popularize mesotherapy. Flack had treatments for a year and claims to have lost forty pounds with the injections. However, she also maintained a diet and exercise plan.

Although mesotherapy has been used in Europe for fifty years, doctors in the United States are concerned about its safety and doubt that the injections are effective. A New Jersey dermatologist and surgeon told *USA Today*, "No one says exactly what they put into the [syringe]. One drug they often use, phosphatidylcholin, is unpredictable and causes extreme inflammation and swelling

People with anorexia, an eating disorder, have an unrealistic view of their bodies and are obsessed with being thin.

where injected. It is not a benign drug." The doctor noted that all dermatologists would be using the injections if they had been proven effective. "If we had something that could [really] melt fat away, it'd be great."[4]

Safety Issues

Whatever the diet products, you might assume that the products have been scientifically tested, that a government agency has placed its stamp of approval on them, and that warning labels for possible side effects are mandatory. But these assumptions are wrong. "None of those protections exist for supplements—only for prescription and over-the-counter medicines," according to *Consumer Reports* magazine, which investigates numerous products. The magazine points out:

> Before approval, drugs must be proved effective, with an acceptable safety profile, by means of lab research and rigorous human clinical trials involving a minimum of several thousand people, many millions of dollars and several years. In contrast, supplement manufacturers can introduce new products without any testing for safety and efficacy. The maker's only obligation is to send the FDA a copy of the language on the label.[5]

In its lengthy report on dietary supplements, *Consumer Reports* explains that even though most probably do no harm, the magazine staff found a dozen supplements that "according to government warnings, adverse-event reports, and top experts are too dangerous to be on the market. Yet they are. We easily purchased all 12 in February [2004] in a few days of shopping online and in retail stores."[6]

Why can dangerous supplements be manufactured and sold in the United States? The case of the now banned weight-loss product ephedra provides one answer. Ephedra is also known as ma huang, a traditional Chinese medicine. Ephedrine alkaloids in the supplements are compounds found in the ephedra species of plants, and they have an amphetamine-type effect—like "uppers." The amount of alkaloids in ephedra-based supplements varies from product to product and an overdose can cause dangerous side effects—even death.

Before the ban, ephedra was widely promoted as the herbal equivalent of "phen-fen," short for a combination of the drugs phentermine and fenfluramine, once used to treat obesity. However, "phen-fen" was banned in 1997 because of its connection to heart problems.

Beginning in the 1990s, the FDA issued warnings about the dangers of the stimulant ephedra in dietary supplements. But the federal Dietary Supplement Health and Education Act (DSHEA) of 1994 requires that the FDA show with certainty that any supplement on the market is unsafe before it can be withdrawn. Although the FDA has tried over the years to investigate consumer complaints about diet products, the agency has been unable in numerous cases to get sufficient information such as lists of ingredients or even samples of supplements. In some instances, the FDA has not been able to identify who manufactured products that users said caused adverse health effects.[7]

Nevertheless, reports continued to show ephedra-linked health problems related to the heart and nervous system, and the FDA finally banned the sale of ephedra in 2004. An advisory from the NIH notes:

> After a careful review of the available evidence about the risks and benefits of ephedra in supplements, the FDA found that these supplements present an unreasonable risk of illness or injury to consumers. The data showed little evidence of ephedra's effectiveness, except for short-term weight loss, while confirming that the substance raises blood pressure and stresses the heart. The increased risk of heart problems and strokes negates any benefits of weight loss.[8]

Internet Claims

Because many people (young and old) surf the Net for information on weight loss, they are especially vulnerable to suggestions that all they have to do is take a pill or potion and fat will fade away. The FDA warns that even though

> the Internet is a rich source of health information, it is also an easy vehicle for spreading myths, hoaxes and rumors about alleged news, studies, products or findings. To avoid falling prey to such hoaxes, be skeptical and watch out for overly emphatic language with

UPPERCASE LETTERS and lots of exclamation points!!!! . . . Ask yourself: Does it sound too good to be true? Do the claims for the product seem exaggerated or unrealistic? Are there simplistic conclusions being drawn from a complex study to sell a product?[9]

Some other safeguards to keep in mind when searching the Web include the following:

- Go to sites of respected organizations such as the American Medical Association, the American Diabetes Association, the American Heart Association, the Mayo Clinic, and the National Institutes of Health.

- Look for nonprofit and government sites that contain no advertising and frequently offer free educational materials.

- Check that the information on a site is written or reviewed by qualified health professionals or experts in the field.

- Be skeptical about testimonials or information from people who have no formal training in nutrition or plants.

- Question health care providers about product benefits claimed by store employees, friends, or people posting on online chat rooms and message boards.

- Think twice about diet supplements that imply they are safe because they are natural products. Some plants, animal extracts, and other substances in nature can be toxic, or poisonous.

- Watch out for sites whose main purpose is to sell a product.

- Check the date of the posted material—perhaps more recent findings are available, especially regarding side effects or interactions with other products.

Buyer Beware

Beyond being cautious about Internet claims and information, there are still other places where a person seeking weight-loss or diet products should be wary: in grocery stores and restaurants. While a decade ago many Americans were buying low-fat foods for weight loss and "heart healthy" diets, today there is a trend (some call it a "craze") for low-carb items. At least one thousand low-carb products have appeared on the market since 2003, and costs of low-carb products are usually higher than others in the same categories. Dieters are spending an average of $85 a month on products labeled low-carb, which in 2004 added up to an estimated total of $25 billion to $30 billion.[10]

Labels on packaged low-carb foods may claim they are "0% carb," "low-carb," "reduced carb," "carb smart," or some other slogan that appeals to dieters. "To capitalize on this low-carb craze, some marketers are touting products as 'no-carb,' even though they never had carbohydrates in them, such as meat products," reports the Partnership for Essential Nutrition. "Others are basically repackaging existing diet or 'lite' products that have been on the market for many years."[11]

In short, a low-carb label "is not what it seems," states the *Wellness Letter* of the University of California at Berkeley. "And any benefits these foods might offer for weight loss or nutrition are debatable, at best. If you replace carbohydrates with protein

Teens should be skeptical about the claims made for weight-loss pills. Most are untested, and many are unsafe.

(that's the main change), you still have just as many calories. Furthermore, the labels are, essentially, meaningless. The FDA has no definition of 'low-carbohydrate' and has never approved any low-carb labels. Any food can be so labeled." The *Letter* ends with this advice:

> Don't be fooled by low-carb foods. There's no evidence that they'll help you lose weight. They are not significantly more nutritious or less caloric than many regular foods. And they eat up food dollars better spent on plain good healthy foods such as fresh fruits and vegetables.[12]

Some fast-food and family restaurants are also on the low-carb bandwagon. McDonald's, Burger King, Wendy's, Subway, Ruby Tuesday, and TGI Friday's are among the well-known chains hyping low-carb meals. But as with packaged foods, low-carb meals may not be as healthy as some regular fare. According to an ABC News report, the Good Housekeeping Institute, working with a laboratory, analyzed food items labeled low-carb on the menus of Ruby Tuesday, TGI Friday's, and Subway. The lab analyzed two items from each of the chains for calories, fat, and carbohydrates, and got

In addition to being cautious about advertising and Internet claims, consumers need to be alert to misleading tactics in grocery stores and restaurants. Some products touted as "low-carb" may not be what they seem.

mixed results. In some cases there were more calories and fat in the meals than described on the menu, because the size of the meal or item and amount of ingredients were larger than expected. Portions often depended on the judgment of the person preparing the food.[13]

Because Americans increasingly eat restaurant meals or other food away from home, the Center for Science in the Public Interest is urging chain restaurants to provide nutritional information for their diners. Some already do on their menus, as just noted, or on their Web sites or in brochures. The center has developed a model menu board for mall food courts and model menus for breakfast, dinner, and pizza restaurants. These models indicate calories, fat, and sodium content for each item offered and are shown in the center's booklet "Anyone's Guess: The Need for Nutrition Labeling at Fast-Food and Other Chain Restaurants."[14]

Legislation has also been introduced in the U.S. Congress to require fast-food outlets and other restaurant chains to inform customers about calories, fat, carbohydrates, and other nutrients. As U.S. Representative Rosa L. DeLauro of Connecticut notes, "I believe people want to make wise choices about what they're eating to have a more healthy diet."[15]

The USDA recommends choosing from a wide variety of nutritious foods and limiting portion sizes in order to lose weight.

To make those "wise choices" while at a restaurant or at home, people also need to be aware of the serving sizes or portions of food they are eating. The USDA food guidelines include recommended serving sizes for someone who needs, for example, 2,000 calories per day. But what is a serving? That varies with each food group. For instance, the guidelines advise eating seven to eight servings, or seven to eight ounces, of whole and other grains daily. Examples of portions that are equivalent to one ounce include one slice of bread, one cup of dry cereal, half a cup of cooked cereal, rice, or pasta. In the milk group, the guidelines suggest three cups each day, which would be equivalent to one cup of low-fat or fat-free milk or yogurt, one half-ounce serving of low-fat cheese, and two ounces of low-fat processed cheese.

Of course, it is not always possible or practical to measure portions before eating, and most of us misjudge the amount of food or beverage we consume, which could easily result in taking in more calories than expected. But those who want to follow recommended servings can keep in mind everyday items to help determine whether they are eating healthy food portions and keeping their calories low. Some examples: half a cup of ice cream is about the size of a tennis ball; a recommended serving of chicken breast or lean meat is similar in size to a deck of cards or the palm of one's hand; vegetable servings may be the size of a baseball. In short, for a healthy diet, the recommended portion size has to be considered along with the number of calories and the nutrient content of foods and beverages.

6   Weight-Loss Surgery

In spite of efforts to avoid fad diets, follow a healthy eating plan, and increase activity, some people simply do not lose weight. Indeed that has been true for numerous adults and young people who are classified as morbidly obese.

What is morbid obesity? The term is applied to those who are extremely overweight—one hundred pounds over their ideal body weight. However, "the accepted definition currently is by BMI, which has to be 40 or above if obesity is the only problem," says Shyam Dahiya, M.D., who specializes in surgical treatment of the morbidly obese at the Bellflower Medical Center in southern California. He adds that people may be seen as morbidly obese if they have a BMI of 35 or higher and also have obesity-related health problems such as sleep apnea, Type II diabetes, or hypertension (high blood pressure).[1]

Someone who is severely obese may suffer from a chronic condition in which symptoms of the problem build slowly. Morbid obesity is then difficult (and sometimes impossible) to treat through diet and exercise alone. After many attempts to lose weight, some morbidly obese people seek a last resort: bariatric surgery, more commonly called weight-loss surgery. The term *bariatric* comes from Greek words meaning "weight" and "treatment."

A study reported in the *JAMA* in October 2004 concluded that such surgery results in weight loss and for some patients also lowers blood pressure and cholesterol and reverses diabetes. However, the researchers did not study the rate of complications from bariatric surgery. "Such problems can include malnourishment (since the stomach is reduced substantially), infections, and a small rate of deaths," according to a report in *BusinessWeek Online*. The report points out that the death rate is less than 1 percent and that "about 10% of patients experience complications" which is in the "expected range for any gastrointestinal surgery."[2]

Bariatric Surgery

Bariatric surgery has been practiced for several decades, but the number of surgeries has increased by ten times since the middle 1990s to about one hundred forty thousand in 2004.[3] Some of the increase may be due to the much-publicized stories of such celebrities as singer and daytime talk show hostess Carnie Wilson, whose surgery in 1999 was televised. She also has published two books on her surgery and weight loss: *Gut Feelings: From Fear and Despair to Health and Hope* (2001) and *I'm Still Hungry: Finding Myself Through Thick and*

Thin (2003). Wilson once weighed 300 pounds and dropped to 150 pounds.

Another well-known TV figure who has called attention to bariatric surgery is Al Roker, the weatherman on the *Today* show. He lost over one hundred pounds after his operation and follow-up with a lean diet and exercise.

Although there are several types of bariatric surgery, basically such an operation decreases the stomach to about the size of an egg so that a person is able to eat less food. The procedure may also rearrange the small intestine so the body absorbs fewer calories. One side effect of weight-loss surgery occurs when patients eat sugary or high-carbohydrate foods. They may experience what is known as the "dumping syndrome"—they feel nauseous, get sweaty, and suffer from diarrhea. Sometimes called the "postop cop," the syndrome helps patients lose weight by discouraging the intake of high-calorie foods and beverages or simply too much food.

Gastric bypass is the most common weight-loss surgery, and involves creating a small stomach pouch and "bypassing" the lower stomach by connecting the pouch directly to the small intestine. Until recent times, this surgery required making a large incision (cut), dividing skin and muscle in the abdomen. Today specialists use a less invasive procedure called laparoscopy, from the Greek words meaning "look into the abdomen." Surgeons use a laparoscope, a pencil-thin optical telescope, inserting it into the abdomen through a small incision. The lightweight, high-resolution video camera allows surgeons to see into the abdomen, explore the whole cavity, and perform the necessary procedures.

Dr. Dahiya at the Bellflower Medical Center notes, "It's a big procedure. You should only have it done if the weight is decreasing your life expectancy and quality of life."[4] Following surgery, a patient achieves the best results when she or he establishes a healthy eating pattern and engages in regular exercise

The singer Carnie Wilson had bariatric surgery and went from 300 to 150 pounds. She is shown here (center) several years after the surgery with the other members of the group Wilson Phillips.

and other physical activities. As the center makes clear, the weight-loss program "is about much more than surgery. It's about a lifelong commitment to a healthier lifestyle." Along with surgeons, specialists from dieticians to physical therapists make up a team at the center that provides direction and support such as nutritional education, meal planning, and exercise guidance for patients.[5]

Banded gastroplasty (or "stomach stapling") has been another common procedure since the 1970s. In this operation, surgeons reduce the size of the stomach with staples (placed like stitches) and a tight plastic band. Stapling the upper stomach creates a small pouch where food goes right after it is swallowed. A synthetic mesh at the outlet of the pouch prevents food from leaving quickly, thus giving a sense of fullness after eating only small amounts. Patients lose weight by eating less at mealtime—provided they do not snack constantly during the rest of the day.

Currently, surgeons can use laparoscopic techniques to implant an adjustable gastric band. The National Library of Medicine explains how an adjustable gastric band works:

> In this procedure, a hollow band made of special material is placed around the stomach near its upper end, creating [a] small pouch and a narrow passage into the larger remaining portion of the stomach. This small passage delays the emptying of food from the pouch and causes a feeling of fullness. The band can be tightened or loosened over time to change the size of the passage. Initially, the pouch holds about 1 ounce of food [five or six bites] and later expands to 2–3 ounces.[6]

How is this device adjusted? A doctor injects or removes fluid from the hollow band, accessing the band through a port, which is a small buttonlike device under the skin in the chest wall. Tubing connects the port to the band. Inflating the band makes the opening smaller, causing food to pass more slowly. Deflating the band does just the opposite, and food passes more quickly.[7]

An experimental procedure to treat overweight patients is a device known as a gastric pacemaker, which is available in Europe but has not yet been approved for use in the United States. Using laparoscopic techniques, a surgeon attaches electrodes to the stomach wall. A wire connects electrodes to the pacemaker—a stimulator that is about the size of a silver dollar. The pacemaker, which is implanted under the skin in the abdomen, sends electrical currents to the stomach. It is not certain exactly what the stimulation does, but researchers say the device may activate hormones that help patients feel full and thus they eat less. Studies on the gastric pacemaker are continuing to determine how the device triggers hormones and what effect they have on weight loss.[8]

Teens and Weight-Loss Surgery

While numerous adults have had gastric bypass surgery over the past decade, that is not the case for adolescents, especially those who are still growing. Usually doctors do not recommend weight-loss surgery for an obese teen unless the young person has obtained full skeletal and sexual growth and may already be suffering adult problems such as arthritis, diabetes, and high blood pressure.

Teenager Raechel Arnold of Claremore, Oklahoma, is an example. In 2003, she weighed 323 pounds, and told a reporter "I had tried exercising, dieting, anything—everything under the sun, I had done. And nothing worked. . . . I played softball and it was getting hard . . . and my feet weren't handling the weight well. . . . It was awful."[9] So after numerous visits with a specialist at a well-known bariatric program at Alvarado Hospital Medical Center in San Diego, California, she underwent surgery. But there were complications. She developed pneumonia in one lung that forced her to stay in the hospital longer than expected. Nevertheless, after returning home she was able within about eight months to lose 140 pounds. Still, that is not the end of her story. She will have to continue a healthy lifestyle program the rest of her life, which includes eating nutritious foods, exercising, and taking vitamin and mineral supplements.

Veronica Salotto of Bellflower, California, is another example. At the age of nineteen, she underwent laparoscopic surgery with Dr. Dahiya performing the operation. Veronica explained that she had been overweight since early childhood and when she bought clothes they had to be the larger sizes. In her words, "At the age of eight, I was wearing about a size twelve in the women's sizes. Going to school wasn't very much fun because not only did I realize I was different but so did my classmates."

Veronica's mother was also overweight and had bariatric surgery in 2002. Her mother suggested that surgery might also help her daughter. As Veronica reports,

> At first I was skeptical, but I began researching a little myself to understand what this surgery was really about. As my mom was going through the pre-operational doctor visits, we attended a few support group meetings. After seeing and hearing so many success stories, I began to realize that this type of surgery might be really good for me.

At the age of seventeen, Veronica decided to meet with Dr. Dahiya, and afterward came to the conclusion that she was too young to make the decision about surgery and was not ready for the procedure. But, she reports,

> two years and frequent doctor visits later, I was well prepared and ready for this. Everything was cleared, and I had my surgery August 9, 2004. . . . This surgery has given me a second chance on my life. . . . I am thankful that I am alive, and I am even more thankful to know that I will be alive much longer than I thought I would be.[10]

Another example of teen weight-loss surgery was featured in *Time* magazine in 2003. The article described the experience of a five-foot-four teenager, Ashlee Townsend, who weighed 330 pounds and had Type II diabetes. Even when she was in third grade, Ashlee had difficulty walking because of her excessive weight, and she often stayed home from school. After surgery, her weight dropped and her diabetes went into remission. But for Ashlee, the most "amazing thing" is "I can see my feet when I walk."[11]

CBS News, ABC News, CNN, and other media outlets have featured teens who have had successful weight-loss surgery as well. Why are teens and their surgeries in the news? Until early in 2004, only about a dozen hospitals in the United States had bariatric surgery programs for teens. But because of long-term health risks

Weatherman Al Roker has also had weight-loss surgery. Here he poses with his wife after losing over 100 pounds.

for morbidly obese youth, more hospitals are considering such programs or have started them. At Tufts-New England Medical Center, a program for adolescents began in January 2004. According to a *Boston Globe* report, Massachusetts General Hospital also offers bariatric surgery for teenagers, and Beth Israel Deaconess Medical Center and UMass Memorial Medical Center are considering doing so. Before teenagers are accepted for surgery at Tufts, they must go through "a six-month screening process during which psychologists, nutritionists, and other health professionals . . . make sure [teenagers have] tried less-drastic measures to lose weight."[12]

In spite of precautions, not all doctors are convinced that bariatric surgery is right for teens. In the Chicago area, pediatric cardiologist David Thoele says, "I think this procedure is a disaster for children. . . . We're giving them an unknown procedure with unknown risks and a risk of death." He recognizes that some extremely obese young people may need surgery, but questions whether parents are looking for a quick-fix way to help their fat kids become thin.[13]

Skeptics contend that there is no guarantee that teen surgeries will be successful just because adults have fared well. There have been no large studies over the long term on what effects bariatric surgery has on teenagers. Only a small number of teens have had the surgery, although no one knows the exact total because there is no tracking system.

Doubters are also concerned about whether teenagers are disciplined enough after surgery to keep up an exercise program and stay away from junk food and other high-calorie items that can stretch the stomach—and add weight. A patient's family has to be willing to be part of the follow-up, which lasts years, helping a young person modify his or her behavior and maintain healthy eating habits and physical activities. Without this family support, the weight-loss surgery cannot be successful, doctors say. "To justify the risk of this operation we have to make sure that we're going to get the support of the family, to maximize the outcome," according to Brian Quebbemann, bariatric surgeon at Hoag Memorial Presbyterian and Huntington Beach hospitals in California. "You don't just treat the child, you treat the parents" as well, he says.[14]

Still other critics question whether teenagers who have bariatric surgery will get enough nutrients in the small amount of food they can eat

> Until very recently, few hospitals offered bariatric surgery for teens. But because of long-term health risks for obese youth, more hospitals have started such programs.

daily. Lack of nutrients could affect growth and learning and perhaps lead to osteoporosis (brittle bones) because of calcium deficiencies.

"Look, kids are not dropping dead at age 19 from obesity," Diana Farmer, M.D., told the *Boston Globe*. Farmer is chief of pediatric surgery at the University of California San Francisco Children's Hospital, and she contends, "Even in obese patients who have diabetes or sleep apnea, there are treatments." She believes that as difficult as it is, adolescents should try to lose weight with diet and exercise and wait until they are adults to decide whether they need and should have bariatric surgery.[15]

The Costs

Whether for teenagers or adults, bariatric surgery is expensive, and the cost can be a significant factor in whether or not the operation takes place. The estimated cost of the operation ranges from about $15,000 up to $50,000, with a price tag of $30,000 often quoted. After surgery, there are additional expenses for years of continued care. Education and counseling regarding diet and exercise can bring the total to about $100,000.

Medical insurance does not necessarily cover this type of operation, unless it is medically necessary—that is, the patient's

BMI is 40 or above or the patient is severely overweight and has life-threatening health problems such as heart disease. In some cases, a person must go through an extensive screening process before insurance coverage is granted. This could include proof that a patient has been through twenty-six weeks of dieting under medical supervision and indications that she or he has the discipline to follow dietary measures required after surgery.

It is not unusual for some insurance companies to turn down patients who want the surgery but are on the borderline of being morbidly obese (for example, someone who has a BMI of 39). Even if patients plan to pay for the surgery, doctors are not likely to perform the operation in this situation.

Some insurance companies will not cover bariatric surgery no matter what the conditions, citing various reasons such as the possibility of medical complications and the "lack of reliable long-term studies of the procedure's success," according to *The Business Journal of Portland*.[16] Insurers also consider bariatric surgery risky, which they blame on the fact that an increasing number of doctors entering the field have little experience or may not be adequately trained in weight-loss surgery. Indeed, some surgeons qualified in other procedures simply announce that they will perform bariatric surgery even though they have little or no training in that area.

While "bariatric surgery is not a specialty certified by the American Board of Surgery or other medical bodies," a doctor certified as a surgeon can enroll in a bariatric seminar or course at a bariatric center, hospital, or institute. "The level of training received by surgeons varies widely, from experiences in residencies or full-fledged yearlong fellowships to weeklong mini-fellowships or brief preceptorships [educational programs] taught by experienced weight-loss surgeons," according to the American Medical Association's *AMNews*.[17]

Other insurers expect a rise in the demand for the surgery in the years ahead, which would lead to higher costs for the insurance companies and a jump in premiums for the insured. For example, Blue Cross Blue Shield of Florida "spent $17 million to cover about 1,000 bariatric surgeries between May 2002 and April 2003, nearly double the amount spent for the like period in 2001–02," according to *AMNews*.[18] The insurer expects those costs to rise significantly during the rest of the decade; as a result, Blue Cross Blue Shield in Florida and Nebraska no longer pay for bariatric surgery.

However, in North Carolina, Blue Cross Blue Shield offers a package of benefits for the insured to help prevent obesity and related health problems. The company will also cover bariatric surgery for the morbidly obese. Although this goes against recent trends, "Other insurance companies and health plans and employers will be watching this very closely," Helen Darling, president of the National Business Group on Health, told the *Washington Post*. The North Carolina insurance benefits include coverage for nutrition counseling and other treatments to prevent weight gain, and if these prove successful, it is likely that insurers and employers in other states will adopt similar insurance programs, Darling predicts.[19]

What About Liposuction?

Liposuction is another type of surgery that technically is part of bariatric medicine, which is concerned with all methods of weight loss. Liposuction is a surgical procedure in which adipose tissue under the skin, which contains fat cells, is broken up and sucked out with a vacuum-like instrument. About four hundred thousand such procedures are performed each year, primarily for cosmetic purposes—to lose flab around the waist, upper arms, buttocks, hips, and other areas.

Until recently, plastic surgeons who performed liposuction touted their procedure as a treatment for obesity, believing it would lower risks for diabetes and heart disease. But a 2004 study shows that liposuction does not affect these risks.

People with questions about weight-loss surgery should speak to a doctor who has experience in the field.

Published in the *New England Journal of Medicine*, the study was led by Samuel Klein, M.D., director of the Center for Human Nutrition at the Washington University School of Medicine in St. Louis, Missouri.

Klein and other researchers expected that removing large amounts of fat—an average of twenty-two pounds—from each of the fifteen obese women in the study would safeguard these patients from high blood pressure, high cholesterol levels, high blood sugar, and other factors that lead to life-threatening diseases. But the researchers found no such benefits. Removing the fat cells under the skin does not have the same effect as losing the fat around internal organs. As Klein explains,

Had these patients lost this much fat by dieting, we would have expected to see marked improvements. Even losing a little fat by dieting—far less than what we removed with liposuction—causes significant [health] benefits. . . . When you lose weight with dieting or exercise, you shrink the size of fat cells, which improves [health]. . . . With liposuction, you remove the number of fat cells, but you don't shrink the size of remaining fat cells.

Klein says the study concludes that diet and exercise are "the way to reduce health risks associated with obesity." In his comments Dr. Klein does not condemn liposuction but instead sees the procedure as having cosmetic benefits that "may stimulate people to become more active, which can help them lose more weight or keep it off. If it achieves that, as it often does with people who get liposuction, that is a good thing."[20]

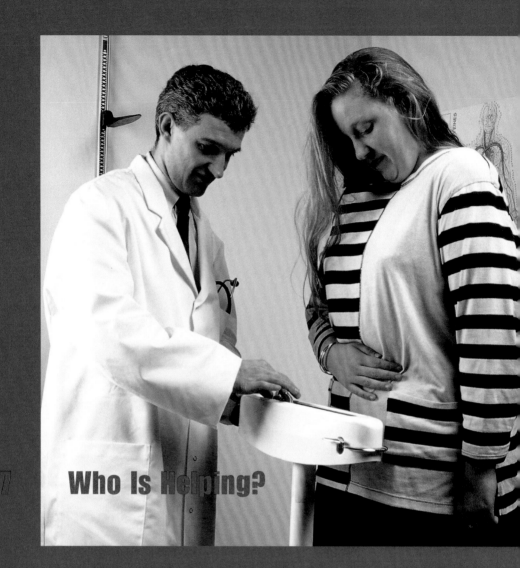

7 **Who Is Helping?**

The television camera pans across a beach, then the screen shows two boys tossing a football along the shore. Suddenly, one of them makes an unusual discovery: a body part seems to be protruding from the sand. As the second boy approaches, he uses a stick to poke at the object and nonchalantly announces that they have come across a human belly. It was probably "lost," he says, by someone running along the beach. The scene plays in various parts of the United States in English and Spanish.

In another TV scene, a man in a mall takes two strange items to the lost-and-found desk. When he drops them off, he asks the clerk what they are and learns he has just found "love handles," or folds of fat. "Lots of people lose them taking the stairs instead of the escalator," says the clerk as he stows the items with other lost articles. A message on the screen advises: "Take the stairs instead of the escalator. Take a small step to get healthy."

In still one more TV spot, a couple pushes a cart through the fresh produce section of a supermarket and bumps into a "double chin" on the floor. The message: Someone lost that extra fat by snacking on fresh fruits and vegetables.

These lighthearted TV incidents are free public service advertisements that were developed by the New York agency McCann Erickson working with the Ad Council and the HHS. The commercials are part of a public awareness campaign to educate Americans that they can take small, achievable steps to improve their health and reverse the obesity trend.

Obesity Prevention Campaigns

In announcing the federal government campaign in March 2004, then HHS Secretary Tommy Thompson said, "We know that gloom and doom messages warning against weight gain don't work. These [media] messages are provocative and attention-getting." Thompson noted that consumers can

> get healthier one small step at a time. Each small step does make a difference, whether it's taking the stairs instead of an elevator or snacking on fruits and vegetables. The more small steps we can take, the further down the road we will be toward better health for ourselves and our families.[1]

The HHS effort is known as the "Healthy Lifestyles and Disease Prevention" initiative and includes a Web site where a visitor can learn more about how to take those small steps toward better health. Another way that HHS and the Ad Council help spread the word about obesity prevention is through *Sesame Street* and its supporting nonprofit organization, Sesame Workshop. *Sesame Street* characters Luis, Elmo, and Rosita encourage parents to make healthier eating and physical activity part of their family's regular routine—as early as possible in their children's lives.

As a part of the federal government's effort to address obesity issues and weight problems, the FDA is preparing guidelines for manufacturers' claims regarding the carbohydrate content of foods. The agency is also revamping regulations for food labels, using larger type to give greater emphasis to calories and serving size. There is already a final FDA rule that requires manufacturers to indicate trans fatty acids (fats that clog arteries) on food labels. In addition, the FDA is working with restaurants to develop a way to include nutrition information on menu items.

In other efforts, the FDA plans to take action against unsafe and falsely labeled dietary supplements. New regulations in the near future will, for the first time, set "manufacturing and labeling standards for all dietary supplements marketed in the United States. These standards will focus on quality, consistency, and potency," says Lester M. Crawford, the FDA's acting commissioner for food and drugs.[2]

Studies Under Way

Research is also part of the strategy to prevent and treat obesity. The NIH, part of HHS, is exploring the many factors that contribute to obesity, such as behavior, culture, economics, environment, and genetics. With hundreds of millions of dollars (more than $440 million in 2005) earmarked for research, the NIH hopes to greatly expand scientific knowledge of this complex and many-sided disorder. *The Strategic Plan for NIH Obesity Research*, released in August 2004, is available free of charge from the Institute.

Whether with the NIH or private laboratories, scientists are at work trying to discover medications that will tackle the obesity problem. Currently only two prescription drugs are available for long-term obesity treatment: Meridia and Xenical.

Meridia suppresses the appetite by affecting control centers in the brain that signal how much a person should eat. Xenical prevents the breakdown of dietary fats into smaller molecules that can be absorbed by the body, and helps eliminate fat through waste products.

Meridia is legally available for adults, but is still being studied for teenagers. Adolescents enrolled in one study reported in the *JAMA* lost weight by taking the drug, but the study cautioned that Meridia does have side effects such as headache, constipation, and insomnia. It can also elevate blood pressure and increase the heart rate.

At the end of 2003, the FDA approved the first drug, Xenical, for treatment of obese teenagers. However, patients who take the drug are advised to also limit high-fat foods such as pizza and French fries and stay on a low-calorie diet. Even then, weight loss is modest, and side effects, such as lack of bowel control, can be uncomfortable and unpleasant.[3]

So far, there are no perfect weight-loss pills or medications that will attack the fat cells in the body. Only in recent times have scientists learned the complexity of fat cells. They make up a network of chemical messengers, and they send out signals to the brain, muscles, liver, and other organs, telling them to act in specific ways. Fat cells are "like little chemical factories continually absorbing or releasing substances in response to the body's energy needs," explains a *Newsweek* report.[4]

Sesame Street characters and TV commercials are trying to get out the message that people can take small, achievable steps to improve their health and reverse the obesity trend.

The complex network of mechanisms and compounds has a profound effect on weight gain and loss that scientists are just beginning to understand. Any drug developed may control one mechanism but not another, so scientists are taking varied approaches as they search for obesity "cures."

In 1994, it seemed that a newly discovered hormone known as leptin could be used to prevent obesity. Leptin, which is produced by fat cells, checks appetite, and it was hoped that it would work as an anti-obesity drug. But scientists have found that in spite of the fact that obese people often have high levels of leptin their bodies resist it. Thus no leptin-based drug has yet been developed for obesity treatment.

However, identifying leptin prompted some scientists to begin research on other hormones that tell the brain to curb the appetite. Other researchers are looking for chemicals that will send a signal from the intestines that a person is full and needs no more food. For example, researchers are studying

Scientists are learning more about the chemistry of food and how our bodies use it. This photograph shows a USDA study of different table spreads and cholesterol.

cholecystokinin, a hormone in the intestine that suppresses appetite; a synthetic form of this hormone taken before meals can fool the body that it has had enough to eat.[5]

One drug, rimonabant, produced by a French company, appears to be promising in human trials. It is known as a CB1 blocker, and it seems to prevent cravings and may control the desire to eat more than needed. Ongoing trials of the drug involve a total of over six thousand obese patients in Europe and the United States. The trials will determine the safety and effectiveness of the drug over a period of at least two years, which is a requirement of the FDA. If approved, the drug could be available in the United States in 2006. Another plus for the drug is its antismoking properties. In separate trials, it has helped smokers quit the habit. In addition, there is evidence that the drug is useful in treating metabolic syndrome, the set of disorders that includes insulin resistance (which can lead to Type II diabetes), high blood pressure, and risk factors for heart disease.[6]

"Rimonabant could prove to be the first bona fide success in years," according to a *BusinessWeek* report.[7] No one expects the medication to be a magical treatment for obesity, but it could be one measure among others that eventually helps some obese patients.

School-Based Programs

Meanwhile, as scientific studies go on, schools and communities are experimenting with programs that are designed to curb overweight and obesity among young people and adults. The National Governors Association points out that teachers, counselors, and other school personnel can help educate students about healthy lifestyles and support nutritious food and beverage choices and regular exercise. Some school efforts, the association says, should include:

- Strengthening physical activity requirements, standards, and programs in schools.

- Implementing nutrition policies and education programs.

- Fostering school and community partnerships that promote regular physical activity.

- Engaging students, school faculty, families, and communities in promoting healthy eating and regular physical activity.[8]

Some states are just beginning to focus on what they can do to help students who are overweight. In Louisiana, for example, where one out of three students is overweight, a state law created a volunteer pilot program beginning in 2005 in eight school districts. Grades seven through ten in eight schools in each district are taking part in the study. Each school follows one of four different plans:

1. Stock at least half of its vending machines with healthy food.

2. Provide increased physical activity.

3. Offer a combination of healthy food and increased physical activity.

4. Do none of the above.

In the fourth plan, the students are a control group. This means that the group is not treated, which allows researchers to compare the other three experimental groups to the control group at the end of the study. Any differences found will theoretically be due to whatever variable (like increased physical activity) has been tested.

The pilot program is designed to determine what strategies work best to help students obtain a healthy weight and lifestyle. At first, some districts and vending machine companies voiced objections because they believed that the state government was trying to regulate what students eat and drink. There were also worries about losing funds from vending sales. But the state hopes the program will show that students can make healthy food choices and that vending sales will not drop.[9]

In schools that are already playing a more active role in helping to reduce childhood obesity, a variety of projects are under way. The Unified School District in San Francisco, California, for instance, has a policy to discourage junk-food sales. A committee of parents, health professionals, and educators developed standards for school foods, which must meet nutrient requirements and be low in sugar and fat.[10]

A two-year prevention program for children in grades three through six in two Chicago schools with African-American populations was conducted by University of Illinois, Chicago, (UIC) graduate students. During the first year in 2002, the emphasis was on helping the children make healthy food choices. The UIC team wrote brief essays about various vegetables and fruits, which included interesting facts about a specific food and information about its origin. The essays were distributed before lunch, which helped increase the consumption of a particular food, according to a report in *Food Service Director*. Students also learned

> how to make more nutritious snacks such as celery stalks topped with peanut butter and chopped raisins. In fact, snacks received a great deal of attention both years, with good reason. Research showed that during any given day many of the students drank four or five 20-ounce sodas and ate bags of chips and salted sunflowers seeds, all of which could be—and often were—purchased at local convenience stores. So in addition to showing the students how to create more healthy snacks from scratch, the UIC students visited the local stores to find specific snack foods they could recommend.[11]

The second year of the program focused on changing behaviors of overweight girls, who were at high risk for obesity, diabetes, and heart disease. The girls volunteered for the experiment and planned their own activities such as walking more each day and eating fewer high-calorie foods.

In Philadelphia, young people at the inner-city Ecology-Technology Academy (EcoTech) are learning about healthy foods by growing them. Because of their families' low incomes, all the students qualify for free lunches, and ordinarily they would eat evening meals at fast-food restaurants several times a week. But that is changing; EcoTech students are studying in the midst of a garden and orchard on a one-acre land parcel. According to a *Newsweek* report, students learn how to grow crops, harvest fruits and vegetables, and sell their produce at a low price to people in their community. When school closes in the summer, they also learn how to cook healthy meals. Some students experience for the first time what fresh foods taste like. As one teenager, Johnathan Russell, noted, "I never had fresh herbs before. It was store-bought all my life. It tastes completely different."[12]

At the other end of the economic scale, in the affluent Ojai Valley School in California, which is a private boarding school and high school, the students seem to understand the concept of eating well. Gina M. Fontana, food service director, says that since she began working in the school food business ten years ago, she has noticed that students at the Ojai School seem to be slimmer than others their age. She explains that vending machines do not offer snacks or soda, only water and Gatorade, and no fast and fried foods are served. At mealtime, students have "a lot of food choices and variety, and they choose more of a plant-based diet and alternative proteins such as soy (tofu, veggie dogs/patties, etc.)." In addition, she says, "I've seen a gradual change in the last couple of years and more so recently. . . . All ground meat has been changed to turkey. . . . The majority of the food choices at our school is organic."

In Fontana's view, when there is a variety of food and it is nutritious, meals are "less expensive. There is much less waste and better health all together." She compares the foods she prepares with those prepared in public schools that receive surplus supplies from the USDA. Officials "will send numerous boxes of canned peaches, huge amounts of processed cheese, etc.—so much that food is wasted. Furthermore, instead of peaches in juice, they provide peaches in syrup. Instead of regular cheese, it's processed," which she believes encourages unhealthy eating.[13]

Community Efforts

Along with schools, entire communities are creating programs to help prevent obesity. An example can be found in the Bootheel

Part of efforts to combat childhood obesity are programs that encourage regular physical activity.

and Ozark areas of Missouri. With CDC support, the St. Louis University Prevention Research Center and the Missouri Department of Health developed and evaluated a physical activity program in rural communities. "Through this program, community coalitions formed walking clubs, built walking trails, started exercise classes in community churches, and organized special events to promote physical activity." What did the program accomplish? An evaluation showed "that 42% of community residents used walking trails established through the program and that almost 60% of trail users increased their physical activity." Another finding: Women and people with lower educational levels—groups that are likely to be physically inactive—"may be especially responsive to walking trails."[14]

In Washington State, projects focus on two communities: Moses Lake and Mount Vernon. Moses Lake is a rural town in eastern Washington where there is a greater percentage of Hispanics, older adults, and people with low incomes than in the rest of the state. These populations are at high risk for obesity-related health problems. The project involves such efforts as improvement of trails, pathways, and sidewalks and creation of bike lanes to encourage physical activity, and development of community gardens to increase fresh fruit and vegetable consumption.

In Mount Vernon, about fifty-five miles from Seattle, with American Indian roots and a population of a little more than twenty-seven thousand, similar projects include efforts to improve active living for older adults and to increase the percentage of young people who walk or bike to school or in their neighborhoods. The city has also developed a diabetes prevention program aimed at American Indians who suffer high rates of this disease.

A community program in New York City called B-Healthy was founded in 2002 by Bryant Terry, whose goal is to call attention to healthy foods by getting young people of color into the kitchen and involved in food preparation. Along with cooking lessons, the African-American and Hispanic teenagers involved can attend classes on such topics as selecting good produce and knowing which vegetables and fruits are in season. They also learn about healthy living. According to a report in *City Limits MONTHLY*,

> B-Healthy's goal is both simple and immense: to cultivate a cadre of young people with a sophisticated understanding of food and nutrition, and who can go out and spread the word. . . . [Terry] hopes to eventually have his students run workshops at after-school programs, at conferences, in front of health and home-ec classes—anyplace where young people gather to learn.[15]

B-Healthy is part of a growing movement across the United States known as "food justice," which is based on the premise that healthy food is a human rights issue. Activists believe that unhealthy lifestyles and overweight problems are often linked to the lack of access to healthy food (processed, high-calorie foods are more available and affordable). Food justice activists attempt to address social, cultural, and economic factors that work against healthy food choices. For example, they may initiate community gardens to help low-income families acquire produce. Or they may work with families to change long-held cooking habits of frying foods in lard and using lots of salt—customs that can lead to weight gain and heart problems.

Although most food justice efforts are not well known, activists hope to increase local production of foods and the number of farmers markets. They also want to organize community groups, particularly in inner cities, that will demand healthy foods and reject processed foods from stores and restaurants—small but important steps toward healthy living.

Although there are many efforts to help Americans establish healthy lifestyles, some people are taking the initiative on their own to lose weight and be more active. And teenagers are among them. A feature about Christianne (described in the first chapter), who was teased by her classmates because of her weight, makes the point. She told *Choices*, "I went to a nutritionist, I went to a personal trainer, my mother tried to help me, my father tried to help me, but nothing worked." She was determined, however, to control her weight and learned about a weight-loss summer camp, which she attended for seven weeks during 2003. With a limited diet and plenty of physical activities, she lost twenty-five pounds. She admits, "I tried to change for other people and I wasn't happy. . . . When I did it for myself, it made it so much easier." Her advice for overweight teens: "Lose weight for yourself, not for someone else."[1]

Other teenagers admit that over time they have usually eaten whatever they wanted and have not exercised, thus becoming heavier. Some who are latchkey kids say they go home from school and immediately hit the refrigerator or cupboards to find snacks—leftovers, candy, chips, or other items—and nibble away until their parents get home. But once some young people realize that they need to change their behavior and lose weight, they may try to adopt a different lifestyle, eating healthier food and getting active.

Changing is not easy, however, and some teenagers have a more difficult time than others losing weight. Yet determination and perseverance do pay off. A slogan that may work for some is: *Focus on your goal, don't give up, and attain the benefits.*

Family Affair

There is little doubt that parents can set examples—positive or negative—for their children's eating habits and exercise routines. On the negative side are parents who do not practice what they preach, demanding physical activity for their youngsters but being couch potatoes themselves. Or parents may encourage unhealthy eating habits by the types of high-calorie foods they prepare and the fast foods they eat. Then there are parents who badger their young children and teenagers about eating too much or deliberately humiliate them about their weight. Repeatedly, young people tell stories about parental harassment that only adds to the frustration and lack of self-respect that overweight young people experience.

On the positive side are supportive parents who protect their overweight children's self-esteem by pointing out that weight is *not* a measure of one's worth but could be a health problem.

Health is foremost at meal and snack time, and for some parents that begins early in their children's lives. One Washington State couple explained that when their son was born, they felt it was important for their child to experience as many varieties of food as possible while growing up. As a result, their son learned to enjoy fresh fruits and vegetables, seafood, poultry, and whole grain foods. Now as a teenager, he prefers healthy food rather than junk food most of the time.

Another important way that parents encourage a healthy lifestyle is at the family dinner table. A family eating a balanced meal together sets an example that can be followed throughout a lifetime. Food service director Gina Fontana at the private Ojai Valley School says she tries to help her fifteen-year-old daughter, who attends a public school, to make better food choices both at home and at school. Fontana says her daughter "is now eating low-fat protein in the morning, more balanced lunches, and a home-cooked dinner. On her own she has decided to try and quit soda. . . . She's replacing soda with water." Fontana adds that her daughter has "always been very physically active and also rides horses almost every day."[2]

Changing is not easy, and some teens have a more difficult time than others losing weight. Yet determination and perseverance do pay off.

An unusual family effort was undertaken by the offspring of Louis S. Yuhasz, better known as "Big Louie," of Alexandria, Virginia. A morbidly obese man at more than five hundred pounds, Big Louie died of complications from a stroke in 2001, which prompted his adult children to do something about obesity. In 2002, they pooled their own money plus donations to create a scholarship fund called "Louie's Kids," and reviewed applications from overweight children and adolescents to attend the Wellspring Adventure Camp in the North Carolina mountains. There campers learn healthy living practices—eating nutritious, low-calorie foods and exercising. During the first year, Louie's Kids awarded three scholarships and did the same in 2003. The following year, the fund provided seven scholarships for needy children, and several came home to boast a weight loss of between fifteen and seventeen pounds.[3]

Physical Activities

Togetherness is also an important factor in physical activity, such as participating in family ball games or taking family bike rides or walks. For example, Susan Hedrick of Nashville, Indiana, a mother who has struggled for most of her life to lose weight, did not want her teenage daughter, Niki, to have the same problem. Hedrick decided that she and her daughter needed to change their sedentary habits and stop eating fast foods. The two now support each other in their efforts to maintain a healthy diet and exercise plan that includes long walks. Both have lost weight, which Niki says she has done "just for my own personal self." Her mom sees their efforts "as a life-changing journey to make myself and Niki healthier."[4]

It may not be a traditional way to get more physical activity, but an increasing number of teenagers are taking part in dance video games that prompt what amounts to an aerobic workout. A popular game is "Dance Dance Revolution," which originated several years ago and is available in a home version as well as in arcades. The home game includes a plastic dance pad with arrows and a video screen with scrolling arrows. Players choose a song and operate the game with their feet, stepping on arrows on the pad that correspond with arrows on the screen. As the song goes on, players move/dance to the beat, which can increase in speed. One teenager who played the game, fourteen-year-old Natalie Henry, did not know she was losing weight until she went to buy new clothes. She found that her regular size was too large. She eventually dropped from

Exercising with friends can be a fun way to stay fit and healthy.

size 14 to size 8. In her words, "The more I played, I gradually had to get smaller-size pants."[5]

Other home video games use motion-sensing technology and a digital camera that allows players to see themselves making karate chops while attacking virtual villains and landing punches in a boxing match. Another game called "Gamebike" was designed by two orthopedic doctors and requires pedaling a bike to control action on a video game. Any bicycle can be used—it is mounted on a standard trainer and the bike is connected to a Playstation video console. In racing games that involve cars, boats, motorcycles, or other vehicles, you pedal as fast as you can to compete. Such games are being used not only at home, but also in hospital exercise programs.[6]

Whether or not you enjoy some type of video game that promotes exercise to lose weight, there are other ways to get up and get moving. As Tommy Thompson, former secretary of HHS, advised young people across America: "Get up and get outdoors. Swim. Hike. Scrimmage. Jog. Skate. Tumble. Sprint. Pirouette. Vault. Dribble. Slam-dunk. Do whatever. Just move your body."[7]

More Suggestions

Countless health care professionals, dieticians, and nutritionists provide other recommendations for weight loss and healthy living. For example, Nissa Beth Gay, a certified nutritionist in California, believes she had an advantage because of the healthy eating habits she learned growing up. While she was young, her parents were vegetarians for several years, which "meant eating lots of tofu, vegetables, and brown rice." Then her family modified the vegetarian diet and began to eat fish on occasion, and insisted on healthy food. "There was never any sugary soda pop in the house, and Twinkies were out of the question." Now in her twenties, Gay believes that for teens, "There is no time better than the present to start watching what you eat. Teenagers have the upper hand because they have plenty of time to change 'not-so-good' eating habits." In her opinion, it is important to control portion sizes and to eat plenty of fruits and vegetables that "will give you more sustained energy to get through the day than any artificial sweets. Breads and other carbohydrates are OK when they are based on whole-wheat flour instead of white flour." In short, she says, "Being a teenager is quite hard and there are so many choices to make. By eating right and exercising, the future becomes much easier as an adult. Trust me, I've been there!"[8]

Eating right is the major emphasis of the American Dietetic Association, which has a Web site that provides dozens of fact sheets on the nutritional values of various foods. The Center for Science and the Public Interest has numerous ideas for healthy eating, such as a *Nutrition Action Healthletter* with a component that compares "right stuff" food (low fat, low calorie) with "food porn" (high fat and calories).

On the USDA's Web site, you can click on an interactive "Healthy Eating Index and Physical Activity Tool." You fill in your daily dietary information or physical activities and you receive a score on the overall quality of your diet or physical activity. The diet score looks at the types and amounts of food you ate as compared to those recommended by the FDA. It also tells you how much total fat, saturated fat (the kind of fat that can lead to heart disease), cholesterol, and sodium you have in your diet. The physical activities score shows the types and duration of each physical activity you did, and then compares this score to the physical activity recommended for health. You can store some information on the site and complete your food intake and physical activity for several days, which gives a better picture of your eating habits or physical activity over time.

Nutritionists and dieticians frequently focus on the importance of reading food labels to determine the calories, nutrients,

Many young people have realized that adopting healthy eating habits
will help them look and feel better.

and other ingredients in a serving size. The serving size is at the top of a label. Below it, the calories and other items are listed per serving. At the bottom of most labels is a list of Daily Values for those who eat 2,000 or 2,500 calories daily. This is a guide to help you get 100 percent of the vitamins and minerals you need each day (from a variety of foods) and to help you cut back on fat, sugar, and sodium (salt) in foods and beverages.

A quick check of a few products indicates a 12-ounce Coke Classic contains 140 calories and 39 grams of sugar. One tablespoon of Hunt's Ketchup has 15 calories and 4 grams of sugar (in the form of high fructose corn syrup and corn syrup, which are sugars nonetheless). A doughnut may have 14 grams of fat compared to a small bagel with 0.5 gram of fat. There are 190 calories in a cup of canned peaches in sugary syrup, but there are only 110 calories in a cup of peaches in natural juice.

In some supermarkets, nutrients and calories are listed on produce shelves for a great variety of fresh fruits and vegetables. The labels on packaged meats, poultry, and fish indicate calories, fat, and protein amounts. The point is knowing the nutrient content of your food helps you make healthy food choices.

What You Can Do

Along with the recommendations for healthy living and weight loss in this chapter, some excellent advice appears in Jay McGraw's *The Ultimate Weight Solution for Teens*. The book is based on the seven keys outlined in the adult book *The Ultimate Weight Solution—The 7 Keys to Weight Freedom* by Jay's father, TV celebrity Dr. Phil McGraw. In addition, the teen book includes journal-like pages for a reader's comments and answers to personal questions.

With the many healthy living suggestions, it is hard to keep everything in mind. So here is a list summarizing some of the points:

- Take responsibility for your food choices and physical activities rather than expect someone else to be your watchdog.

- Plan for the long term, not quick fixes.

- Set realistic goals.

- Pat yourself on the back for trying, rather than blame yourself or your heritage for your body image.

- Ask your family and/or friends to support you as you establish healthy eating and exercise habits.

- Go back to your routine and drop the guilt trip if you stray on occasion.

- Limit your time watching TV, playing video games, and using the computer.

- Investigate and choose nutritious snacks; ask family members, nutritionists, dieticians, or health care providers for advice.

- Keep a journal to remind yourself about your progress.

- Avoid comparing yourself to celebrities who supposedly have "ideal" bodies but may not be healthy.

Finally, remember an important tip that worked for Christianne (and no doubt many other people): Strive to be healthy for yourself, not for someone else.

Chapter Notes

Chapter 1   What Is Obesity?

1. Denise Rinaldo, "Weight War," *Choices*, April–May 2004, p. 8.
2. Julia Sommerfeld, "Teen Weight-Loss Surgery: Is Benefit Worth The Risk?" *Seattle Times*, December 16, 2003, <http://seattletimes. nwsource.com/html/health/135178879_obesekids07m0.html> (August 7, 2004).
3. National Institute of Diabetes and Digestive and Kidney Diseases, National Institutes of Health, "Statistics Related to Overweight and Obesity," July 2003, <http://win.niddk.nih.gov/statistics/index. htm> (June 30, 2004).
4. MedlinePlus Medical Encyclopedia, "Obesity," June 22, 2004, <http://www.nlm.nih.gov/medlineplus/ency/article/003101.htm> (June 30, 2004).
5. "Headed for Heart Attacks? Doctors Fear Obese Teens May Not Outlive Their Parents," *ABCNEWS.com*, June 3, 2004, <http:// abcnews. go.com/sections/GMA/DrJohnson/Obesity_teens_ health_040603.html> (June 29, 2004).
6. Ibid.
7. WIN Weight-control Information Network, National Institute of Diabetes and Digestive and Kidney Diseases, "Statistics Related to Overweight and Obesity," October 6, 2004, <http://win.niddk.nih. gov/statistics/index.htm> (January 30, 2005); see also National Center for Health Statistics, "Prevalence of Overweight Among Children and Adolescents: United States, 1999-2000," <http://www. cdc.gov/nchs/products/pubs/pubd/hestats/overwght99.htm> (January 30, 2005).
8. Greg Bonnell, "Study Sounds New Obesity Alert," *Toronto Star*, June 15, 2004, <http://www.axisoflogic.com/cgi-bin/exec/view.pl? archive=63&num=9127> (June 29, 2003); see also "The Canadian Community Health Survey," *The Daily*, June 14, 2004, <http:// www.statcan.ca/Daily/English/040615/d040615b.htm> (June 29, 2004).

9. Rob Stein, "CDC Study Overestimated Deaths From Obesity," *Washington Post*, November 24, 2004, p. A11.

10. Centers for Disease Control and Prevention, "BMI—Body Mass Index: BMI for Children and Teens," n.d., <http://www.cdc.gov/nccdphp/dnpa/bmi/bmi-for-age.htm> (January 31, 2005); see also Centers for Disease Control and Prevention, "2000 CDC Growth Charts: United States,"<http://www.cdc.gov/nchs/about/major/nhanes/growthcharts/background.htm> (January 31, 2005).

11. Center for Consumer Freedom, "No Increase in Obesity Numbers, Despite Panicky Headlines," June 21, 2004, <http://www.consumerfreedom.com/about.cfm> (June 30, 2004).

12. Glenn A. Gaesser, *Big Fat Lies: The Truth About Your Weight and Your Health* (Carlsbad, Calif.: Gürze Books, 2002), p. xiii.

13. Daniel Q. Haney, "Medical World Debates Risk of Being Pudgy," *WashingtonPost.com*, June 28, 2004, <http://www.washingtonpost.com/wp-dyn/articles/A11630-2004Jun28.html> (July 11, 2004).

14. Amanda Spake, "Rethinking Weight," *U.S. News & World Report*, February 9, 2004, p. 56.

15. Steven N. Blair and Tim S. Church, "The Fitness, Obesity, and Health Equation: Is Physical Activity the Common Denominator?" extract, *Journal of the American Medical Association*, pp. 1232–1234, September 8, 2004, <http://jama.ama-assn.org/cgi/content/extract/292/10/1232> (September 8, 2004).

16. Gina Kolata, "The Fat Epidemic: He Says It's an Illusion," *New York Times*, June 8, 2004, p. F5.

Chapter 2   Causes of Obesity

1. Amanda Spake, "Rethinking Weight," *U.S. News & World Report*, February 9, 2004, p. 53.

2. Shahrad Taheri, Ling Lin, Diane Austin, Terry Young, and Emmanuel Mignot, "Short Sleep Duration Is Associated with Reduced Leptin, Elevated Ghrelin, and Increased Body Mass Index," *Public Library of Science*, December 2004, <http://medicine.plosjournals.org/perlserv/?request=get-document&doi=/10.1371/journal.pmed.0010062#N107> (May 21, 2005); see also: "Sleep Deprivation Tied to Shifts in Hunger Hormones,"

ScientificAmerican.com, December 7, 2004, <www.sciam.com/article.cfm?articleID=00042C19-D5B3-11B4-95B383414B7 F0000> (May 21, 2005).

3. Kevin Patrick, Gregory J. Norman, Karen J. Calfas, James F. Sallis, Marion F. Zabinski, Joan Rupp, and John Cella, "Diet, Physical Activity, and Sedentary Behaviors as Risk Factors for Overweight in Adolescence," *Archives of Pediatric Adolescent Medicine*, April 2004, pp. 385–390.

4. Jeanie Lerche Davis, "Exercise Reverses Obese Kids' Heart Disease," *WebMD Medical News*, April 5, 2004, <http://my.webmd.com/content/Article/85/98470.htm> (February 1, 2005).

5. U.S. Department of Health and Human Services, "Physical Activity Fact Sheet," n.d., <http://fitness.gov/physical_activity_fact_sheet.html> (July 5, 2004).

6. Richard Lacayo, "The Walking Cure," *Time*, June 7, 2004, p. 97.

7. Centers for Disease Control and Prevention, "Participation in High School Physical Education—United States, 1991–2003," *Morbidity and Mortality Weekly Report*, September 17, 2004, <http://www.cdc.gov/mmwr/preview/mmwrhtml/mm5336a5.htm> (February 1, 2005); see also "More Schools Benching P.E.," *CNN.com*, January 18, 2005, <http://www.cnn.com/2005/EDUCATION/01/18/pitiful.physed.ap/index.html> (January 18, 2005).

8. Aileo Weinmann, "Schools Eye Cuts in Gym Classes to Save Money," Capital News Service, Michigan State University School of Journalism, October 10, 2003, <http://www.cns.jrn.msu.edu/articles/2003_1010/PHYSEDCUTS.html> (July 12, 2004).

9. Kelly D. Brownell and Katherine Battle Horgen, *Food Fight: The Inside Story of the Food Industry, America's Obesity Crisis, and What We Can Do About It* (Chicago: Contemporary Books, 2004), p. 36.

10. Marion Nestle, *Food Politics: How the Food Industry Influences Nutrition and Health* (Berkeley: University of California Press, 2002), p. 13.

11. Ibid., p. 25.

12. Mary Story and Simone French, "Food Advertising and Marketing Directed at Children and Adolescents in the US," *International*

Journal of Behavioral Nutrition and Physical Activity, February 10, 2004, <http://www.ijbnpa.org/content/1/1/3> (July 8, 2004).

13. Washington State Department of Health, "Teen Health and the Media," n.d., <http://depts.washington.edu/thmedia/view.cgi?section=bodyimage> (July 12, 2004).

14. Shanthy A. Bowman, Steven L. Gortmaker, Cara B. Ebbeling, Mark A. Pereira, and David S. Ludwig, "Effects of Fast-Food Consumption on Energy Intake and Diet Quality Among Children in a National Household Survey," *Pediatrics*, January 2004, pp. 112–118.

15. "International Survey: Fattest Teens in U.S.," *CNN.com*, January 6, 2004, <http://www.cnn.com/2004/HEALTH/parenting/01/05/obese.teens.ap/> (July 8, 2004).

16. "Lean Teens More Likely To Compensate For Overeating Than Overweight Peers," *Health & Medicine Week*, July 5, 2004, p. 809; See also Cara B. Ebbeling, Kelly B. Sinclair, Mark A. Pereira, Erica Garcia-Lago, Henry A. Feldman, David S. Ludwig, "Compensation for Energy Intake From Fast Food Among Overweight and Lean Adolescents," *Journal of the American Medical Association*, June 16, 2004, <http://jama.ama-assn.org/cgi/content/abstract/291/23/2828> (July 8, 2004).

17. National Conference of State Legislatures, "Vending Machines in Schools," June 30, 2004, <http://www.ncsl.org/programs/health/vending.htm> (July 11, 2004).

18. Center for Science in the Public Interest, "Dispensing Junk: How School Vending Undermines Efforts to Feed Children Well," May 2004, p. 1, <http://cspinet.org/new/pdf/dispensing_junk.pdf> (July 11, 2004).

19. Centers for Science in the Public Interest, "School Vending Machines 'Dispensing Junk,'" Press Release, May 11, 2004, <http://cspinet.org/new/20040511.html>

20. Greg Critser, *Fat Land: How Americans Became the Fattest People in the World* (Boston: Houghton Mifflin Company, 2003), p. 48.

21. "School Vending Machines Losing Favor," *CNN.com*, July 14, 2003, <http://www.cnn.com/2003/EDUCATION/07/14/food.vending.reut> (July 11, 2004).

Chapter 3 Health Risks and Costs

1. National Institute of Diabetes and Digestive and Kidney Diseases of the National Institutes of Health, "Understanding Adult Obesity," October 2001, <http://win.niddk.nih.gov/publications/understanding.htm> (February 2, 2005).

2. American Diabetes Association, "All About Diabetes," n.d., <http://www.diabetes.org/about-diabetes.jsp> (July 16, 2004).

3. National Institute of Diabetes and Digestive and Kidney Diseases, "Study Will Identify Best Treatment for Type 2 Diabetes in Youth," Press Release, March 15, 2004, <http://www.niddk.nih.gov/welcome/releases/03-15-04.htm> (July 16, 2004).

4. American Diabetes Association, "Diabetes Statistics for Youth," n.d., <http://www.diabetes.org/diabetes-statistics/children.jsp> (July 17, 2004).

5. Lisa Greene, "Diagnosis Diabetes—Special Report on an American Epidemic," *St. Petersburg Times*, April 18, 2004, pp. 1A, 8–10A.

6. Ibid.

7. University of Rochester Medical Center, "1 Million Teens at Risk for Diabetes and Heart Disease," Press Release, August 11, 2003, <http://www.urmc.rochester.edu/pr/news/story.cfm?id=349> (July 14, 2004).

8. Lester M. Crawford, D.V.M., Ph.D., Speech before the National Medical Association House of Delegates Meeting, San Diego, California, August 4, 2004, <http://www.fda.gov/oc/speeches/2004/nma0804.html> (August 22, 2004).

9. U.S. Centers for Disease Control and Prevention, "Overweight children and adolescents 6–19 years of age, according to sex, age, race, and Hispanic origin: United States, selected years 1963–65 through 1999–2000," January 14, 2003, <http://www.cdc.gov/nchs/data/hus/tables/2002/02hus071.pdf> (July 14, 2004).

10. "In the Southeast, a Costly Appetite," *AARP Bulletin*, April 2004, p. 25.

11. Bethany Spicher, "Toward Food Justice," *Sojourners Magazine*, July 2004, p. 8.

12. Tracie McMillan, "The Action Diet: The Food Justice Movement Looks To Change More Than Just What New York Kids Eat," *City*

Limits MONTHLY, July–August 2004, p. 20; also available <http://www.citylimits.org/content/articles/articleView.cfm?articlenumber=1156> (August 22, 2004).

13. Karen Ann Cullotta, "Cure to Child Obesity May Be Nearby Grocery Store," *Chicago Tribune*, March 28, 2004, Section 2, p. 2.

14. Callie Lyons, "Poverty Foils Healthy Food Choices," *The Marietta Times*, July 16, 2003, <http://www.mariettatimes.com/news/story/0716202003_new01obeisty.asp> (July 15, 2004).

15. U.S. Centers for Disease Control and Prevention, "Obesity Costs States Billions in Medical Expenses," Press Release, January 21, 2004, <http://www.cdc.gov/od/oc/media/pressrel/r040121.htm> (July 16, 2004).

16. Crawford.

17. National Institute of Diabetes & Digestive & Kidney Diseases, National Institutes of Health, "Obesity in Youth Leads to Increased Economic Costs," *WIN Notes*, Winter 2002/2003, p. 5, <http://www.niddk.nih.gov/health/nutrit/winnotes/winter03notes/obesity.htm> (July 17, 2004).

Chapter 4 What About Weight-Loss Diets?

1. University of Pittsburgh Medical Center, "Fad Diets," 2003, <http://patienteducation.upmc.com/Pdf/FadDiets.pdf> (July 24, 2004).

2. Glenn A. Gaesser, Ph.D., *Big Fat Lies: The Truth About Your Weight and Your Health* (Carlsbad, Calif.: Gürze Books, 2002), p. 29.

3. American Academy of Family Physicians, "Fad Diets: What You Need to Know," *familydoctor.org*, February 2004, <http://familydoctor.org/x6629.xml> (July 24, 2004).

4. Partnership for Essential Nutrition, "Low-Carbohydrate Diets," n.d., <http://www.essentialnutrition.org/lowcarb.php> (July 23, 2004).

5. "Q&A: Dr. Robert Eckel on Nutrition," *ABCNews.com*, May 22, 2003, <http://abcnews.go.com/sections/community/WorldNewsTonight/chat_eckel030522.html> (July 24, 2004).

6. Jamie Cohen, "Analyzing Atkins Diet," *ABCNews.com*, May 21,

2003, <http://abcnews.go.com/sections/living/WorldNewsTonight/
Atkinsstudies_030521.html> (July 24, 2004).

7. "Weight Watchers Announces New Position On Enrollment of
   Children and Adolescents," Press Release, March 31, 2003,
   <http://www.weightwatchers.com/about/prs/wwi_template.aspx?
   GCMSID=1003161> (July 27, 2004).

8. Kathleen Doheny, "Teens and Dieting a Losing Proposition,"
   HealthDay, April 2, 2004, <http://www.hon.ch/News/HST/517559.
   html> (July 26, 2004).

9. Ibid.

10. Jean A. Welsh, Mary E. Cogswell, Sharmini Rogers, Helaine
    Rockett, Zuguo Mei, and Laurence M. Grummer-Strawn,
    "Overweight Among Low-Income Preschool Children Associated
    With the Consumption of Sweet Drinks: Missouri, 1999–2002,"
    Pediatrics, February 2005, pp. e223–e229.

Chapter 5 More Diet Dangers

1. Kevin Zhou, "The Flawed Media Coverage of Teen Obesity,"
   Online NewsHour, September 29, 2003,
   <http://www.pbs.org/newshour/extra/speakout/editorial/obesity_
   9-29.html> (July 27, 2004).

2. "Diets and Dollar Signs" (chart), *MSNBC.com*, August 31, 2004,
   <http://www.msnbc.msn.com/id/4139024/> (August 31, 2004).

3. "Diet Pills Promise Rapid Weight Loss, With Faulty Tactics,"
   ABCNews.com, April 23, 2004, <http://www.abcnews.go.com/
   sections/2020/Living/2020_diet_ads_040423.html>
   (July 30, 2004).

4. Maria Puente, "Critics Worried About Latest Weight-Loss Fad,"
   Indianapolis Star, August 8, 2004, <http://www.indystar.com/
   articles/7/168566-8147-P.html> (August 10, 2004).

5. "Dangerous Supplements: Still at Large," *Consumer Reports*, May
   2004, p. 14.

6. Ibid., p. 12.

7. Janet Raloff, "Diet Pills: It's Still Buyer Beware," *Science News
   Online*, August 10, 2002, <http://www.sciencenews.org/articles/
   20020810/food.asp> (July 30, 2004).

8. National Center for Complementary and Alternative Medicine, National Institutes of Health, "Ephedra," April 19, 2004, <http://nccam.nih.gov/health/alerts/ephedra/consumeradvisory.htm> (July 30, 2004); see also FDA News, "FDA Issues Regulation Prohibiting Sale of Dietary Supplements Containing Ephedrine Alkaloids and Reiterates Its Advice That Consumers Stop Using These Products," Press Release, February 6, 2004, <http://www.cfsan.fda.gov/~lrd/fpephed6.html> (July 30, 2004).

9. U.S. Food and Drug Administration Center for Food Safety and Applied Nutrition, "Tips for the Savvy Supplement User: Making Informed Decisions And Evaluating Information," January 2002, <http://www.cfsan.fda.gov/~dms/ds-savvy.html> (July 30, 2004).

10. Partnership for Essential Nutrition, "The Skinny on Low-Carb Claims," June 2004, <http://www.essentialnutrition.org/claims.php> (July 31, 2004).

11. Ibid.

12. "Low-Carb Foods Less Than Meets the Eye," *UC Berkeley Wellness Letter*, January 2004, <http://www.berkeleywellness.com/html/wl/2004/wlFeatured0104.html> (August 1, 2004).

13. "Low-Carb Fast Foods May Not Be the Healthiest Choice," *ABCNews.com*, January 21, 2004, <http://abcnews.go.com/sections/GMA/living/Atkins_fast_food_040121.html> (August 1, 2004).

14. Center for Science in the Public Interest, "Anyone's Guess: The Need for Nutrition Labeling at Fast-Food and Other Chain Restaurants" (booklet), November 2003, <www.cspinet.org/restaurantreport.pdf> (February 4, 2005).

15. "Nutrition Labels for Fast Foods," National Public Radio, November 10, 2003, <http://www.npr.org/features/feature.php?wfId=1497083> (August 1, 2004).

Chapter 6 Weight-Loss Surgery

1. Shyam Dahiya, M.D., e-mail correspondence with the author, August 3, 2004.

2. Amy Tsao, "Battling Obesity: Weighing Bariatric Surgery's Risks," *Business Week Online*, October 28, 2004, <http://www.businessweek.

    com/bwdaily/dnflash/oct2004/nf20041028_0264_db092.htm>
(January 30, 2005).

3. Ibid.

4. Sue Vorenberg, "Weighty Decision," *Albuquerque Tribune*, April 8, 2004, <http://www.abqtrib.com/archives/news04/040804_news_gastric.shtml> (August 6, 2004).

5. Bellflower Medical Center, "Weight Loss Surgery A Lifelong Decision," pamphlet, n.d.

6. MedlinePlus, National Library of Medicine, National Institutes of Health, "Adjustable Gastric Banding," January 29, 2003, <http://www.nlm.nih.gov/medlineplus/ency/imagepages/19497.htm> (August 6, 2004).

7. U.S. Food and Drug Administration, "New Device Approval," June 4, 2001, <http://www.fda.gov/cdrh/mda/docs/p000008.html> (August 6, 2004).

8. "Implantable Gastric Pacemaker to Aid Weight Loss," *Medical News Today*, December 31, 2003, <http://www.medicalnewstoday.com/index.php?newsid=5086#> (August 22, 2004); see also Anita P. Courcoulas, "The Evolution of Surgery for Obesity: Past, Present, and Future," *Spotlight Health*, June 1, 2004, <http://www.spotlighthealth.com/nasp/beyond_change/moarticle.asp?article_id=80> (August 22, 2004).

9. Nanci Hellmich, "Raechel Arnold: Slimmer, Healthier, Happier," *USA Today*, July 27, 2004, <http://www.usatoday.com/news/health/2004-07-27-teens-bypass_x.htm> (August 7, 2004).

10. Veronica Salotto, e-mail to the author, August 15, 2004.

11. Christine Gorman, "Desperate Measures: As a Last Resort, More and More Obese Teens Are Having Their Stomachs Stapled," *Time*, November 17, 2003, p. 58.

12. Liz Kowalczyk, "Surgery on Rise for Obese Teens," *Boston Globe*, January 13, 2004, <http://www.boston.com/business/articles/2004/01/13/surgery_on_rise_for_obese_teens> (August 8, 2004).

13. Sylvia Perez, "Teen Obesity: A Drastic Solution," *ABC7Chicago.com*, November 6, 2003, <http://abclocal.go.com/wls/news/110203_ss_teenobesity.html> (August 8, 2004).

14. Debbie Talanian, "Young People Opt For Bariatric Surgery," *The*

Post & Courier, March 3, 2003, <http://www.charleston.net/stories0/030303/sci_03bari.shtml> (August 8, 2004).

15. Kowalczyk.

16. Robin J. Moody, "Insurance Carriers Leery of Paying For Bariatric Surgery," *The Business Journal of Portland*, August 25, 2003, <http://portland.bizjournals.com/portland/stories/2003/08/25/story4.html> (August 9, 2004).

17. Robert Kazel, "Insurers Trim Bariatric Surgery Coverage," *AMNews*, April 5, 2004, <http://www.ama-assn.org/amednews/2004/04/05/bil20405.htm> (August 10, 2004).

18. Ibid.

19. Rob Stein, "N.C. Health Insurer to Offer Coverage for Weight Problems," *Washington Post*, October 13, 2004, p. A02

20. Sid Kirchheimer, "Risks from Obesity Same After Liposuction," *WebMD*, June 17, 2004, <http://my.webmd.com/content/Article/89/100118.htm> (August 10, 2004); see also Denise Grady, "Liposuction Doesn't Offer Health Benefit, Study Shows," *New York Times*, June 17, 2004, p. A24.

Chapter 7   Who Is Helping?

1. U.S. Department of Health and Human Services, "Citing 'Dangerous Increase' in Deaths, HHS Launches New Strategies Against Overweight Epidemic," Press Release, March 9, 2004.

2. Lester M. Crawford, Speech before National Medical Association House of Delegates Meeting, San Diego, California, August 4, 2004, <http://www.fda.gov/oc/speeches/2004/nma0804.html> (August 18, 2004).

3. Anahad O'Connor and Denise Grady, "F.D.A. Moves to Let Drug Treat Obese Teenagers," *New York Times*, December 16, 2003, <http://www.nytimes.com/2003/12/16/health/16FAT.html?ex=1093320000&en=66eef92c2eead60f&ei=5070> (August 22, 2004).

4. Anne Underwood and Jerry Adler, "What You Don't Know about Fat," *Newsweek*, August 23, 2004, p. 40; See also Rob Stein, "Decoding the Surprisingly Active Life Of Fat Cells," *Washington Post*, July 12, 2004, p. A1.

5. Alice Park, "Pills in the Pipeline," *Time*, June 7, 2004, p. 90.

6. Drug Development Technology, "Acomplia (Rimonabant)— Investigational Agent For The Management Of Obesity," 2005, <http://www.drugdevelopment-technology.com/projects/rimonabant/> (February 7, 2005).

7. Amy Taso, "Has Obesity Met Its Match?" *BusinessWeek Online*, April 8, 2004, <http://www.businessweek.com/print/technology/content/apr2004/tc2004048_9548_tc122.htm?tc> (August 19, 2004).

8. National Governors Association, "Preventing Obesity in Youth through School-Based Efforts," Issue Brief, February 4, 2003, <http://www.nga.org/cda/files/022603PREVENTING.pdf> (July 28, 2005).

9. "Louisiana Passes Bill To Study Childhood Obesity," *Network of Care for Children and Family Services*, August 9, 2004, <http://fresno.networkofcare.org/family/news/detail.cfm?articleID=5719> (August 22, 2004).

10. Katherine Shek, "Expert: Schools Should Increase Role in Fighting Obesity," *Education Daily*, July 22, 2004, p. 6.

11. Susie Stephenson, "Healthy Kids 101: University of Illinois Nutrition Professor Pioneers Obesity Intervention Efforts in Chicago Elementary Schools," *Food Service Director*, July 15, 2004, p. 34.

12. Peg Tyre and Julie Scelfo, "Helping Kids Get Fit: Communities Are Finding New Ways for Youngsters to Trim Down and Tone Up," *Newsweek*, September 22, 2003, p. 60.

13. Gina Fontana, e-mail to the author, September 4, 2004.

14. U.S. Department of Health and Human Services, "Preventing Chronic Diseases: Investing Wisely in Health Preventing Obesity and Chronic Diseases Through Good Nutrition and Physical Activity," August 2003, <http://www.cdc.gov/nccdphp/pe_factsheets/pe_pa.htm> (August 16, 2004).

15. Tracie McMillan, "The Action Diet: The Food Justice Movement Looks to Change More than Just What New York Kids Eat," *City Limits MONTHLY*, July–August 2004, p. 19; also available at <http://www.citylimits.org/content/articles/articleView.cfm?articlenumber=1156> (August 17, 2004).

Chapter 8 Healthy Lifestyles

1. Denise Rinaldo, "Weight War: Growing Numbers of Teens in the United States Are Overweight, and the Problem Keeps Getting Bigger," *Scholastic Choices*, April–May 2004, p. 9.
2. Gina Fontana, e-mail to the author, September 4, 2004.
3. Annie Gowen, "From Family's Pain, Hope for Obese Youths," *Washington Post*, September 6, 2004, p. A1.
4. "Generations Team Up to Fight the Fat, Get Fit," *St. Petersburg Times*, July 6, 2004, p. 3A.
5. Anita Chang, "Video Game Gets Players In Shape With Dance Moves," *Detroit Free Press*, June 10, 2004, <http://www.freep.com/news/health/ddr10_20040610.htm> (July 13, 2004).
6. Margaret Bernstein, "Interactive Games Put Kids in Motion While They're Playing," *Cleveland Plain Dealer*, April 24, 2004, <http://www.cleveland.com/living/plaindealer/index.ssf?/base/living/1082817000323540.xml> (August 23, 2004).
7. National Institute of Diabetes & Digestive & Kidney Diseases, National Institutes of Health, "Obesity in Youth Leads to Increased Economic Costs," *WIN Notes*, Winter 2002/2003, p. 5 <http://www.niddk.nih.gov/notes/winter03notes/obesity.htm> (July 17, 2004).
8. Nissa Beth Gay, e-mail to the author, August 26, 2004.

Glossary

body mass index (BMI)—A standard for measuring whether weight points to a health problem.

calorie—A measurement of the fuel, or energy, produced in the body.

carb—Abbreviation for carbohydrate.

carbohydrate—A source of energy found in foods.

cholesterol—Fatlike substance in the blood.

diabetes—A disease in which the body does not make enough insulin or does not use it efficiently.

fat cell—A cell in which energy is stored in the body.

insulin—A hormone that regulates glucose (sugar) levels in the blood.

legumes—Food plants with pods such as beans and lentils.

metabolic syndrome—Set of characteristics that can lead to the early onset of diabetes and also heart disease.

protein—Basic substance of body cells.

triglycerides—Blood fats that increase the risk of heart disease.

For More Information

American Diabetes
Association
1701 North Beauregard Street
Alexandria, Va. 22311
800-342-2383

American Heart Association
National Center
7272 Greenville Avenue
Dallas, Tex. 75231
800-242-8721

American Obesity
Association
1250 24th Street, NW
Suite 300
Washington, D.C. 20037
202-776-7711

Center for Consumer
Freedom
P.O. Box 27414
Washington, D.C. 20038
202-463-7112

Centers for Disease Control
and Prevention
1600 Clifton Road
Atlanta, Ga. 30333
404-639-3311

Mayo Clinic
200 First Street, S.W.
Rochester, Minn. 55905
507-284-2511

National Institutes of
Health
9000 Rockville Pike
Bethesda, Md. 20892
301-496-4000

Further Reading

Abramovitz, Melissa. *Obesity*. San Diego, Calif.: Lucent Books, 2004.

Gedatus, Gus. *Exercise for Weight Management*. Mankato, Minn.: Lifematters, 2001.

Johnson, Susan, and Laurel Mellin. *Just For Kids! Obesity Prevention Workbook*. San Anselmo, Calif.: Balboa Publishing Company, 2002.

Levy, Lance. *Understanding Obesity*. Buffalo, New York: Firefly Books, 2000.

Libal, Autumn, and Ellyn Sanna, *America's Unhealthy Lifestyle: Supersize It!* Philadelphia: Mason Crest Publishers, 2004.

Owens, Peter. *Teens: Health & Obesity*. Philadelphia: Mason Crest Publishers, 2005.

Vogel, Shawna. *The Skinny on Fat*. New York: W. H. Freeman, 1999.

Internet Addresses

American Dietetic Association
   <http://www.eatright.org>

Center for Science in the Public Interest
   <http://www.cspinet.org>

Food Pyramid, U.S. Department of Agriculture
   <http://www.mypyramid.gov>

Index